Julia High Performance
Second Edition

Optimizations, distributed computing, multithreading, and
GPU programming with Julia 1.0 and beyond

Avik Sengupta

D1282065

BIRMINGHAM - MUMBAI

Julia High Performance
Second Edition

Commissioning Editor: Aaron Lazar
Acquisition Editor: Denim Pinto
Content Development Editor: Akshita Billava
Technical Editor: Neha Pande
Copy Editor: Safis Editing
Project Coordinator: Vaidehi Sawant
Proofreader: Safis Editing
Indexer: Tejal Daruwale Soni
Production Designer: Jisha Chirayil

First published: April 2016
Second edition: June 2019

Production reference: 1070619

Published by Packt Publishing Ltd.
Livery Place
35 Livery Street
Birmingham
B3 2PB, UK.

ISBN 978-1-78829-811-7

www.packtpub.com

To Vaishali and Ahan—for whom I do everything that I do.

— Avik Sengupta

Packt.com

Subscribe to our online digital library for full access to over 7,000 books and videos, as well as industry leading tools to help you plan your personal development and advance your career. For more information, please visit our website.

Why subscribe?

- Spend less time learning and more time coding with practical eBooks and Videos from over 4,000 industry professionals

- Improve your learning with Skill Plans built especially for you

- Get a free eBook or video every month

- Fully searchable for easy access to vital information

- Copy and paste, print, and bookmark content

Did you know that Packt offers eBook versions of every book published, with PDF and ePub files available? You can upgrade to the eBook version at www.packt.com and as a print book customer, you are entitled to a discount on the eBook copy. Get in touch with us at customercare@packtpub.com for more details.

At www.packt.com, you can also read a collection of free technical articles, sign up for a range of free newsletters, and receive exclusive discounts and offers on Packt books and eBooks.

Foreword

Those who are new to Julia often ask me what makes it so special, or how it achieves such high performance. Having to think on my feet in order to answer this question has proven challenging. This was the case, at least, until Avik Sengupta came along with the *Julia High Performance* book. Now all I have to do is tell the enquirers to read the book as it consists of just the right combination of details to answer their questions.

In an easy-to-read concise set of chapters - most of which contain words like "performance" and "fast" - Avik takes you through examples that you can run yourself in order to see how fast and easy Julia is to use.

There are computer science words that have become Julia words. It is a pleasure to learn these in a manner that is easy to follow. Just a few examples of this are "JIT", "Multiple Dispatch", "type system", "generated functions", "CUDA", and "SIMD".

After learning about Julia's design, you will learn to measure performance. From there, you will appreciate Julia's type system. You will then master using arrays along with making fast function calls and fast numbers. Finally, you will learn to write parallel Julia programs.

With *Julia High Performance,* you'll pick up the key essentials of Julia in no time. You can then join the friendly, fast growing, online community of Julia programmers.

Welcome to the world of Julia! Read this book and you will soon join us in *loving* the Julia language.

Alan Edelman
Professor of Applied Mathematics
Computer Science & AI Labs Member
MIT
Co-creator, The Julia Language

Contributors

About the author

Avik Sengupta is the vice president of engineering at Julia Computing, a contributor to open source Julia, and the maintainer of several Julia packages. Avik is the co-founder of two start-ups in the financial services and AI sectors, and is a creator of large, complex trading systems for the world's leading investment banks. Prior to Julia Computing, Avik was co-founder and CTO at AlgoCircle and at Itellix, director at Lab49, and head of algorithmic solutions at Decimal Point Analytics. Avik earned his MS in computational finance at Carnegie Mellon and MBA Finance at the Indian Institute of Management in Bangalore.

This book wouldn't exist, and my life would have been very different, if, almost over a decade ago, four people across the world did not imagine that scientific computing needed a new language. Thank you, Jeff, Alan, Viral, and Stefan, for launching a thousand ships.

My colleagues at Julia Computing have been a source of immense support. Among others, Keno Fischer, Matt Bauman, Kristoffer Carlson, and Tanmay Mohapatra have helped clear my misconceptions, and have provided code and ideas that have seeped into this book. I'm also grateful to my reviewers, who've painstakingly provided detailed feedback on this book. All of them have made this book immeasurably better, but the responsibility for any errors, of course, remains my own.

And finally, a word of thanks to the entire Julia community. The depth and breadth of knowledge and skill I have encountered are exceptional. Over the past few years, I've learned so much—things that I should have known, and things that I never thought I could know. Thank you for sharing your knowledge so generously.

About the reviewers

Lyndon White is a research engineer at Invenia Labs, living in Broadway Nedlands, Australia. His key research areas include natural language processing and computational linguistics, with a focus on the capturing of sentence meaning. More broadly, his interests include machine learning, data mining, pattern recognition, and artificial intelligence. His overarching goal is to develop methods to allow for better computational processing of vast amounts of data intended for manual (human) processing via media such as books, blogs, and newspapers. He gained a bachelor's degree in engineering (electrical and electronic) and a bachelor's degree in computer and mathematical science from the University of Western Australia in 2014, where he continued his PhD studies.

Zhuo Qingliang (also known as KDr2 online) is presently working at paodingai.com, a start-up FinTech company in China that is dedicated to improving the financial industry by using artificial intelligence technologies. He has over 10 years of experience in Linux, C, C++, Python, Perl, and Java development. He is interested in programming, doing consulting work, and participating in and contributing to the open source community (including the Julia community, of course).

Packt is searching for authors like you

If you're interested in becoming an author for Packt, please visit authors.packtpub.com and apply today. We have worked with thousands of developers and tech professionals, just like you, to help them share their insight with the global tech community. You can make a general application, apply for a specific hot topic that we are recruiting an author for, or submit your own idea.

Table of Contents

Preface

The Julia programming language has brought an innovative new approach to scientific computing, promising a combination of performance and productivity that is not usually available in the current set of languages that is commonly used. In solving the two-language problem, it has seen tremendous growth both in academia and industry. It has been used in domains from robotics, astronomy, and physics, to insurance and trading. It has particular relevance in the area of machine learning, with increasing use for the emerging field of differentiable computing.

Most new developers are attracted to the language due to its promise of high performance. This book shows you how and why that is possible. We talk about the design choices of the language's creators that allow such a high-performance compiler to be built. We also show you the steps that you, as an application developer, can take to ensure the highest possible performance for your code. We also tell you the ways in which your code can work with the compiler and runtime to fully utilize your hardware to the greatest extent possible.

Who this book is for

This book is for the beginner and intermediate Julia developer who wants to fully leverage Julia's promise of performance with productivity. We assume you are proficient with one or more programming languages and have some familiarity with Julia's syntax. We do not expect you to be expert Julia programmers yet but assume that you have written small Julia programs, or that you have taken an introductory course on the language.

What this book covers

Chapter 1, *Julia is Fast*, is your introduction to Julia's unique performance. Julia is a high-performance language, with the possibility to run code that is competitive in performance with code written in C. This chapter explains why Julia code is fast. It also provides context and sets the stage for the rest of the book.

Chapter 2, *Analyzing Performance*, shows you how to measure the speed of Julia programs and understand where the bottlenecks are. It also shows you how to measure the memory usage of Julia programs and the amount of time spent on garbage collection.

Chapter 3, *Types, Type Inference, and Stability,* covers type information. One of the principal ways in which Julia achieves its performance goals is by using type information. This chapter describes how the Julia compiler uses type information to create fast machine code. It describes ways of writing Julia code to provide effective type information to the Julia compiler.

Chapter 4, *Making Fast Function Calls,* explores functions. Functions are the primary artifacts for code organization in Julia, with multiple dispatch being the single most important design feature in the language. This chapter shows you how to use these facilities for fast code.

Chapter 5, *Fast Numbers,* describes some internals of Julia's number types in relation to performance, and helps you understand the design decisions that were made to achieve that performance.

Chapter 6, *Using Arrays,* focuses on arrays. Arrays are one of the most important data structures in scientific programming. This chapter shows you how to get the best performance out of your arrays—how to store them, and how to operate on them.

Chapter 7, *Accelerating Code with the GPU,* covers the GPU. In recent years, the general-purpose GPU has turned out to be one of the best ways of running fast parallel computations. Julia provides a unique method for compiling high-level code to the GPU. This chapter shows you how to use the GPU with Julia.

Chapter 8, *Concurrent Programming with Tasks,* looks at concurrent programming. Most programs in Julia run on a single thread, on a single processor core. However, certain concurrent primitives make it possible to run parallel, or seemingly parallel, operations, without the full complexities of shared memory multi-threading. In this chapter, we discuss how the concepts of tasks and asynchronous IO help create responsive programs.

Chapter 9, *Threads,* moves on to look at how Julia now has new experimental support for shared memory multi-threading. In this chapter, we discuss the implementation details of this mode, and see how this is different from other languages. We see how to speed up our computations using threads, and learn some of the limitations that currently exist in this model.

Chapter 10, *Distributed Computing with Julia,* recognizes that there comes a time in every large computation's life when living on a single machine is not enough. There is either too much data to fit in the memory of a single machine, or computations need to be finished quicker than can be achieved on all the cores of a single processor. At that stage, computation moves from a single machine to many. Julia comes with advanced distributed computation facilities built in, which we describe in this chapter.

To get the most out of this book

This book has been written to be a practical guide to improving the performance of your Julia code. As such, we encourage you to run the code shown in this book yourself. Running the code and inspecting the output for yourself is the best way to learn the methods suggested here. All the code is available in machine-readable format (see the following for download instructions), so we suggest having a Julia REPL open while you read this book, so that you can copy and paste code on to it.

Download the example code files

You can view and download all code for this book at `https://juliahighperformance.com`.

You can download the example code files for this book from your account at `www.packt.com`. If you purchased this book elsewhere, you can visit `www.packt.com/support` and register to have the files emailed directly to you.

You can download the code files by following these steps:

1. Log in or register at `www.packt.com`.
2. Select the **SUPPORT** tab.
3. Click on **Code Downloads & Errata**.
4. Enter the name of the book in the **Search** box and follow the onscreen instructions.

Once the file is downloaded, please make sure that you unzip or extract the folder using the latest version of:

- WinRAR/7-Zip for Windows
- Zipeg/iZip/UnRarX for Mac
- 7-Zip/PeaZip for Linux

The code bundle for the book is also hosted on GitHub at `https://github.com/PacktPublishing/Julia-High-Performance-Second-Edition`. In case there's an update to the code, it will be updated on the existing GitHub repository.

We also have other code bundles from our rich catalog of books and videos available at `https://github.com/PacktPublishing/`. Check them out!

Download the color images

We also provide a PDF file that has color images of the screenshots/diagrams used in this book. You can download it here: https://www.packtpub.com/sites/default/files/downloads/9781788298117_ColorImages.pdf.

Code in Action

Click on the following link to see the Code in Action: http://bit.ly/2WsMomd

Conventions used

There are a number of text conventions used throughout this book.

CodeInText: Indicates code words in text, function or method names, folder names, and filenames. Here is an example: "Mount the downloaded WebStorm-10*.dmg disk image file as another disk in your system."

A block of code is set as follows:

```
struct Pixel{T}
    x::Int64
    y::Int64
    color::T
end
```

When we wish to draw your attention to a particular part of a code block, the relevant lines or items are set in bold:

```
function sum_cols_matrix(x)
   num_cols = size(x, 2)
   s = zeros(num_cols)
   for i = 1:num_cols
      s[i] = sum_vector(x[:, i])
   end
   return s
end
```

Most code snippets in this book have been typed at the Julia REPL. This is denoted by the `julia>` prompt. Such a listing will show the output of the expression below the expression itself. If you type the code into the REPL yourself, this is exactly what you should see:

```
julia> a = fill(1, 4,4)
4×4 Array{Int64,2}:
 1 1 1 1
 1 1 1 1
 1 1 1 1
 1 1 1 1
```

Bold: Indicates a new term, an important word, or words that you see onscreen. For example, words in menus or dialog boxes appear in the text like this. Here is an example: "Select **System info** from the **Administration** panel."

Warnings or important notes appear like this.

Tips and tricks appear like this.

Get in touch

Feedback from our readers is always welcome.

General feedback: If you have questions about any aspect of this book, mention the book title in the subject of your message and email us at customercare@packtpub.com.

Errata: Although we have taken every care to ensure the accuracy of our content, mistakes do happen. If you have found a mistake in this book, we would be grateful if you would report this to us. Please visit www.packt.com/submit-errata, selecting your book, clicking on the Errata Submission Form link, and entering the details.

Piracy: If you come across any illegal copies of our works in any form on the Internet, we would be grateful if you would provide us with the location address or website name. Please contact us at copyright@packt.com with a link to the material.

If you are interested in becoming an author: If there is a topic that you have expertise in and you are interested in either writing or contributing to a book, please visit authors.packtpub.com.

Reviews

Please leave a review. Once you have read and used this book, why not leave a review on the site that you purchased it from? Potential readers can then see and use your unbiased opinion to make purchase decisions, we at Packt can understand what you think about our products, and our authors can see your feedback on their book. Thank you!

For more information about Packt, please visit packt.com.

1
Julia is Fast

In many ways, the history of programming languages has been driven by, and certainly intertwined with, the needs of numerical and scientific computing. The first high-level programming language, Fortran, was created to solve scientific computing problems, and continues to be important in the field even to this day. In recent years, the rise of data science as a specialty has brought additional focus to numerical computing, particularly for statistical uses. In this area, somewhat counter-intuitively, both specialized languages such as R and general-purpose languages such as Python are in widespread use. The rise of Hadoop and Spark has spread the use of Java and Scala respectively among this community. In the midst of all this, Matlab has had a strong niche within engineering communities, while Mathematica remains unparalleled for symbolic operations.

A new language for scientific computing therefore has a very high barrier to overcome, and it's been only a few short years since the Julia language was introduced to the world. In that time, however, its innovative features, combining the ease of use of a dynamic language and the performance of a statically compiled language, have created a growing niche within the numerical computing world. Based on multiple dispatch as its defining paradigm, Julia is a very pleasant language to program in, making mathematical abstractions very easy to express. However, it was the claim of high performance that drew the earliest adopters.

This, then, is a book that celebrates writing high-performance programs. With Julia, this is not only possible, but also reasonably straightforward, in a low-overhead, dynamic language.

As a reader of this book, you have likely already written your first few Julia programs. We will assume that you have successfully installed Julia, and have a working programming environment available. We expect you are familiar with very basic Julia syntax, but we will discuss and review many of those concepts throughout the book as we introduce them.

In this chapter, we will describe some of the underlying design elements of Julia that contribute to its well-deserved reputation as a fast language:

- Julia – fast and dynamic
- Designed for speed
- How fast can Julia be?

Julia – fast and dynamic

It is a widely believed myth in programming language communities that high-performance languages and dynamic languages are completely disjointed sets. The perceived wisdom is that, if you want programmer productivity, you should use a dynamic language, such as Ruby, Python, or R. On the other hand, if you want fast code execution, you should use a statically typed language, such as C or Java.

There are always exceptions to this rule. However, for most mainstream programmers, this is a strongly held belief. This usually manifests itself in what is known as the two-language problem. This is something that is especially prominent in scientific computing. This is the situation where the performance-critical inner kernel is written in C, but is then wrapped and used from a dynamic, higher-level language. Code written in traditional, scientific computing environments such as R, Matlab, or NumPy follows this paradigm.

Code written in this fashion is not without its drawbacks, however. Even though it looks like it gets you the best of both worlds—fast computation, while allowing the programmer to use a high-level language—this is a path full of hidden dangers. For one, someone will have to write the low-level kernel. So, you need two different skill sets. If you are lucky enough to find the low-level code in C for your project, you are fine. However, if you are doing anything new or original, or even slightly different from the norm, you will find yourself writing both C and a high-level language. This will severely limit the number of contributors that your projects or research will get: to be really productive, those contributors really have to be familiar with two languages.

Secondly, when running code routinely written in two languages, there can be severe and unforeseen performance pitfalls. When you can drop down to C code quickly, everything is fine. However, if, for time reasons, effort, skill or changing requirements, you cannot write a performance-intensive part of your algorithm in C, you'll find your program taking hundreds or even thousands of times longer than you expected.

Julia is the first modern language to make a reasonable effort to solve the two-language problem. It is a high-level, dynamic language with powerful features that make for very productive programming. At the same time, code written in Julia usually runs very quickly, almost as quickly as code written in statically typed languages.

The rest of this chapter describes some of the underlying design decisions that make Julia such a fast language. We'll also look at some evidence of the performance claims about Julia. The rest of the book shows you how to write your Julia programs to be as fast and lean as possible. We will discuss how to measure and reason about performance in Julia, and how to avoid some potential performance roadblocks.

For all the content in this book, we will usually illustrate our points with small, self-contained programs. We hope that this will enable you grasp the crux of the issue, without getting distracted by unnecessary elements of a larger program. We expect that this methodology will therefore provide you with instinctive intuition about Julia's performance profile.

Julia has a refreshingly simple performance model—thus, writing fast Julia code is a matter of understanding a few key elements of computer architecture, and how the Julia compiler interacts with it. We hope that, by the end of this book, your instincts are developed well enough to design and write your own Julia code with the fastest possible performance.

Finally, Julia will work for you at both ends of the compute spectrum. On one hand, its performance and expressiveness allows it to run embedded use cases on low-powered processors and it is fully supported on ARM processors, and works well on the Raspberry Pi, which makes it a perfect environment for teaching programming. At the other end of the spectrum, Julia has been used to run large-scale machine learning applications on some of the world's largest super-computers. The Celeste project used Julia Build and Atlas of the Sky, where the computation ran at an amazing 1.5 petaflops (1 petaflop is 10^{15} floating point operations per second, or a thousand million million), using 1.3 million threads. This was the first time any dynamic language had broken the petaflop barrier. So, Julia can run on machines large and small, scaling massively in both directions.

Versions of Julia:

The code and examples in this book are targeted at version 1.2 of the language, which is the most recently released version at the time of publication. Since there will be no breaking changes in the 1.x series of Julia, most of the code in this book should work on version 1.0 onward, which was released in August of 2018.

Designed for speed

When the creators of Julia launched the language into the world, they said the following in a blog post entitled *Why We Created Julia*, which was published in early 2012:

> *"We want a language that's open source, with a liberal license. We want the speed of C with the dynamism of Ruby. We want a language that's homoiconic, with true macros like Lisp, but with obvious, familiar mathematical notation like Matlab. We want something as usable for general programming as Python, as easy for statistics as R, as natural for string processing as Perl, as powerful for linear algebra as Matlab, as good at gluing programs together as the shell. Something that is dirt simple to learn, yet keeps the most serious hackers happy. We want it interactive and we want it compiled. (Did we mention it should be as fast as C?)"*

High-performance, indeed nearly C-level performance, has therefore been one of the founding principles of the language. It's built from the ground up to enable the fast execution of code.

In addition to being a core design principle, it has also been a necessity from the early stages of its development. A very large part of Julia's standard library, including very basic low-level operations, is written in Julia itself. For example, the + operation to add two integers is defined in Julia itself. (Refer to: `https://github.com/JuliaLang/julia/blob/e1def102429941705bc16009e35a74abcdb6f88e/base/int.jl#L38`.) Similarly, the basic `for` loop uses the standard iteration mechanism available to all user-defined types. Broadcasting, which is a fundamental low-level operation in the compiler, can be completely overridden by custom array types (this is used heavily in CUDA arrays, for example). All of this means that the compiler had to be very fast from the very beginning to create a usable language. The creators of Julia did not have the luxury of escaping to C for even the core elements of the library.

We will note throughout the book the many design decisions that have been made with an eye to high performance, but there are three main elements that create the basis for Julia's speed: a high performance Just in Time compiler, LLVM to generate machine code, and a type system that allows expressive code.

JIT and LLVM

Julia is a **Just In Time** (JIT) compiled language, rather than an interpreted one. This allows Julia to be dynamic, without having the overhead of interpretation. This compilation infrastructure is built on top of **LLVM**—more information about it is available on its website: `http://llvm.org`.

The LLVM compiler infrastructure project originated at the University of Illinois. It now has contributions from a very large number of corporate as well as independent developers. As a result of all this work, it is now a very high-quality, yet modular, system for many different compilation and code generation activities.

Julia uses LLVM for its JIT compilation needs. The Julia runtime code generator produces LLVM **Intermediate Representation (IR)** and hands it over to LLVM's JIT compiler, which in turn generates machine code that is executed on the CPU. As a result, sophisticated compilation techniques that are built into LLVM are ready and available to Julia, from simple ones (such as *Loop Unrolling* or *Loop Deletion*) to state-of-the-art ones (such as *SIMD Vectorization*). These compiler optimizations form a very large body of work and, in this sense, the existence of LLVM is very much a pre-requisite to the existence of Julia. It would have been an almost impossible task for a small team of developers to build this compiler and code generation infrastructure from scratch.

Just-In-Time compilation:
A technique in which the code in a high-level language is converted to machine code for execution on the CPU at runtime. This is in contrast to interpreted languages, whose runtime executes the source language directly.

This usually has a significantly higher overhead. On the other hand, **Ahead of Time (AOT)** compilation refers to the technique of converting a source language into machine code as a separate step prior to running the code. In this case, the converted machine code can usually be saved to disk as an executable file.

Types, type inference, and code specialization

While LLVM provides the basic infrastructure that allows fast machine code to be produced, it must be noted that adding an LLVM compiler to any language will not necessarily make it execute faster. Julia's syntax and semantics have been carefully designed to allow high-performance execution, and a large part of this is due to how Julia uses types in the language. We will, of course, have much more to say about types in Julia throughout this book. At this stage, suffice it to say that Julia's concept of types is a key ingredient of its performance.

The Julia compiler attempts to infer the type of all data used in a program, and compiles different versions of functions specialized to particular types of its arguments. To take a simple example, consider the ^ (power) function. This function can be called with integer or floating point (i.e, fractional, or decimal) arguments. The mathematical definitions and, thus, the implementation of this function are very different for integers and floats. So, Julia will compile, on demand, two versions of the code, one for integer arguments, and one for floating point arguments, and insert the appropriate call in the code when it compiles the program. This means that, at runtime, fast, straight-line code without any type checks will be executed on the CPU.

Julia allows us to introspect the native code that runs on the CPU. Using this facility, we can see that very different code is generated for integer and floating point arguments. So, let's look at the following machine code, generated for squaring an integer:

```
julia> @code_native 3^2
  pushl %eax
  decl %eax
  movl $202927424, %eax ## imm = 0xC186D40
  addl %eax, (%eax)
  addb %al, (%eax)
  calll *%eax
  popl %ecx
  retl
```

 We omitted some boilerplate output when showing the result of the @code macros, in order to focus on the relevant parts. Run this code yourself to see the full output.

Let's now look at the following code, generated for squaring a floating point value:

```
julia> @code_native 3.5^2
  vcvtsi2sdl %edi, %xmm1, %xmm1
  decl %eax
  movl $1993314664, %eax ## imm = 0x76CF9168
  .byte 0xff .byte 0x7f .byte 0x00
  addb %bh, %bh
  loopne 0x68
  nopw %cs:(%eax, %eax)
```

You will notice that the code looks very different (although the actual meaning of the code is not relevant for now). You will notice that there are no runtime type checks in the code. This gets to the heart of Julia's design and its performance claims.

The ability of the compiler to reason about types is due to the combination of a sophisticated dataflow-based algorithm, and careful language design that allows this information to be inferred from most programs before execution begins. Put in another way, the language is designed to make it easy to statically analyze its data types.

If there is a single reason for Julia being such a high-performance language, this is it. This is why Julia is able to run at C-like speeds while still being a dynamic language. *Type inference* and *code specialization* are as close to a secret sauce as Julia gets. It is notable that, outside this type inference mechanism, the Julia compiler is quite simple. It does not include many of the advanced *Just in Time* optimizations that Java and JavaScript compilers are known to use. When the compiler has enough information about the types within the code, it can generate optimized, straight-line code without many of these advanced techniques.

 Detailed information about the implementation of type inference and code specialization in Julia can be found in the paper *Julia: A Fresh Approach to Numerical Computing*. Jeff Bezanson, Alan Edelman, Stefan Karpinski, and Viral B. Shah (2017) *SIAM Review*, 59: 65–98. doi: `10.1137/141000671`. URL: `https://julialang.org/research/julia-fresh-approach-BEKS.pdf`

It is useful to note here that, unlike some optionally typed dynamic languages, simply adding type annotations to your code does not make Julia go any faster. Type inference means that the compiler is usually able to figure out the types of variables when necessary. Hence, you can usually write high-level code without fighting with the compiler about types, and still achieve superior performance.

How fast can Julia be?

The best evidence of Julia's performance claims is when you write your own code. We encourage you to run and measure all the code snippets in the book. To start, we will provide an indication of how fast Julia can be by comparing a similar algorithm on multiple languages.

As an example, consider the algorithm to compute a Mandelbrot set. Given a complex number, z, the function computes whether, after a certain number of iterations, the $f_c(z) = z^2 + c$ function converges or not. Plotting the imaginary numbers where that function diverges on a 2D plane produces the following iconic fractal image that is associated with this set:

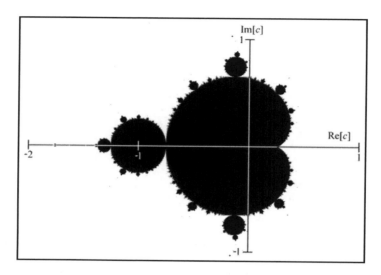

The following code computes the divergence point based on this logic. Calling this function over all points on a 2D plane will produce the Mandelbrot set:

```
function mandel(c)
    z = c
    maxiter = 80
     for n in 1:maxiter
        if abs(z) > 2
             return n - 1
        end
        z = z^2 + c
    end
    return maxiter
end
```

You will notice that this code contains no type annotations, or any special markup, even though it operates on complex numbers. It looks remarkably clean, and the idea that the same mathematical operations can apply to many different kinds of mathematical objects is key to Julia's expressiveness.

The same algorithm implemented in modern C would look as follows:

```
int mandel(double complex z) {
    int maxiter = 80;
    double complex c = z;
    for (int n = 0; n < maxiter; ++n) {
        if (cabs(z) > 2.0) {
            return n;
        }
        z = z*z+c;
    }
    return maxiter;
}
```

Downloading the example code:
You can download the example code files for this book from your account at http://www.packtpub.com. If you purchased this book elsewhere, you can visit http://www.packtpub.com/support and register to have the files emailed directly to you.

You can download the code files by taking the following steps:

1. Log in or register on our website using your email address and password
2. Let the mouse pointer hover over the SUPPORT tab at the top
3. Click on Code Downloads & Errata
4. Enter the name of the book in the Search box
5. Select the book for which you're looking to download the code files
6. Choose from the drop-down menu where you purchased this book
7. Click on Code Download

Once the file is downloaded, please make sure that you unzip or extract the folder using the latest version of the following:

- WinRAR/7-Zip for Windows
- Zipeg/iZip/UnRarX for Mac
- 7-Zip/PeaZip for Linux

By timing this code in Julia and C, as well as re-implementing it in many other languages (all of which are available within the *Microbencmarks* project at `https://github.com/JuliaLang/Microbenchmarks`), we can note that Julia's performance claims are certainly borne out for this small program. Plotting these timing results in the following chart, we see that Julia can perform at a level similar to C and other statically typed and compiled languages:

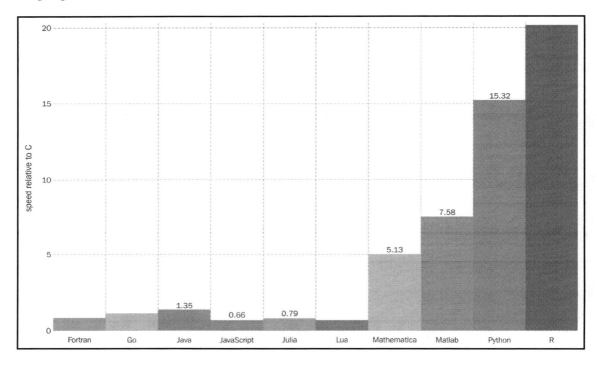

This is, of course, a micro benchmark, and therefore cannot be extrapolated too much. However, I hope you will agree that it is certainly possible to achieve exceptional performance in Julia, without having to fall back to low-level languages for performance-critical code. The rest of the book will attempt to show how we can achieve performance close to this standard, for many different kinds of code bases. We will learn how to squeeze the maximum possible performance from the CPU, without any of the overhead that typically plagues dynamic languages.

Summary

In this chapter, we noted that Julia is a language that is built from the ground up for high performance. Its design and implementation have always been focused on providing the highest possible performance on a modern CPU.

The rest of the book will show you how to use the power of Julia fully, to write the fastest possible code in this language. In the next chapter, we will discuss how to measure the speed of Julia code, and identify performance bottlenecks. You will also learn about some of the tools that are built into Julia for this purpose.

Analyzing Performance

2

The aim of this book is to show us how to improve the performance of our Julia code, but before we can improve, we must measure. To try and optimize any Julia code we have written, we first need to understand its performance characteristics. Is the code fast enough for our needs? If not, is there an upper limit to how fast it can be? And finally, can we understand where the bottlenecks are, so that we can prioritize where to focus our efforts. This chapter will show us the tools available in Julia to answer these questions and more. In later chapters, we will see how to use this information to improve our code.

In this chapter, we will cover the following topics:

- Timing Julia functions
- Accurate benchmarking
- Profiling Julia functions
- Tracking detailed memory allocation

Timing Julia functions

The first step to understanding anything is to measure it. The same goes for writing high-performance Julia code. We need to measure the performance of the code as the first step to achieving that. As a high-performance language, Julia includes many tools to do this easily, effectively, and accurately. Many of these are built into the language and the standard library, while others are in external packages that can be installed with a single command. All of these tools not only make it easy to measure the performance of the code; they also make it easy to execute the measurement correctly.

When reading this book, whether in print or on screen, we encourage you to run the code and see the results for yourself. The concepts in this book will become much easier to learn if you run the code yourself. The simplest would be to copy/paste the code you see in this book into the Julia REPL.

The REPL (or the Read-Eval-Print-Loop, aka the Julia> prompt) is what you get when you run the Julia executable. It is the best command-line environment you will have seen, with features such as full history, multiline editing, and multiple modes. The code that you see in this book is written as if entered on the REPL. And in an amazing feat of user friendliness, you can copy and paste the entire line, including the text of the prompt (in other words, the julia> text). Upon pasting, the REPL will recognize this, and do the right thing. Do try this!

The @time macro

Whenever you care about the performance of your code, the @time macro will end up being one of your most widely used commands on the Julia prompt. Built into the base Julia runtime, this macro wraps the provided expression to calculate and print the elapsed time while running it. It also measures and prints the amount of memory allocated while running that code.

```
julia> @time sqrt(rand(1000));
 0.000023 seconds (8 allocations: 15.969 KB)
```

Any kind of Julia expressions can be wrapped by the @time macro. Usually, it is a function call as above, but it could be any other valid expression:

```
julia> @time for i in 1:1000
           x = sin.(rand(1000))
       end
 0.023210 seconds (2.00 k allocations: 15.503 MiB, 38.35% gc time)
```

Timing measurements and JIT compiling:
Recall that Julia is a JIT-compiled language. This means that the Julia compiler and runtime compiles any Julia code into machine code the first time it sees it. This means that, if you measure the execution time of any Julia expression that executes for the first time, you will end up measuring the time (and memory use) required compiling this code. So, whenever you time any piece of Julia code, it is crucial to run it at least once prior to measuring the execution time. Always measure the second or later invocation.

Other time macros

An enhanced version of the @time macro is also available; this is the @timev macro. This macro operates in a manner very similar to @time, but measures some additional memory statistics, and provides elapsed time measurements to nanosecond precision. The following output shows the result of running this macro:

```
julia> @timev sqrt.(rand(1000));
  0.000012 seconds (8 allocations: 15.969 KB)
elapsed time (ns): 11551
bytes allocated:    16352
pool allocs:        6
non-pool GC allocs:2
```

Both the @time and @timev macros return the value of the expression whose performance they measured (note the semicolon at the end of the preceding expression—this prevents the REPL from outputting the return value to the console). Hence, these can be added without side effects to almost any location within the Julia code.

They can be used to measure the performance of the specific expression we are interested in, and still use the computed value for further operations. For example, it could be used within a function call's arguments. In the following expression, the @time macro is used to time the execution of the sqrt function, and then the result of that function is passed as an argument to the sum function:

```
julia> sum(@time sqrt.(rand(1000)))
0.000373 seconds (29 allocations: 17.047 KiB)
656.069185135439
```

`@elapsed` is yet another built-in macro that can be used to measure the execution time of Julia programs. Unlike the `@time` or `@timev` macros, which output the time information to the console, the `@elapsed` macro returns the time in seconds as a result:

```
julia> @elapsed sqrt.(rand(1000))
0.000217478
```

This means that these resulting times can be used for further processing—for example, they can be used to assert performance limits during unit testing:

```
julia> using Test

julia> @test @elapsed(sqrt.(rand(1000))) <= 10e-4
Test Passed
```

These macros are useful to measure the performance of individual expressions. To fully understand how larger codebases perform, we need a profiler.

The Julia profiler

The Julia runtime includes a built-in profiler, which can be used to measure how long each line of code takes to run, relative to a certain code base. It can therefore be used to identify bottlenecks in code, which can, in turn, be used to prioritize optimization efforts.

This built-in system implements what is known as a **sampling profiler**. As its name suggests, it samples the program call stack at certain points in time. When the profiler is run, it stops and inspects the running system every few milliseconds (by default, 1 millisecond on UNIX, and 10 milliseconds on Windows). At every point, the profiler identifies the list of function calls (and the line of code they originate), from the start of the program to the current point, and updates a counter for every line it sees on the call stack. The idea is that the lines of code that are executed most are also found more often on the call stack. Hence, over many such samples, the count of how often each line of code is encountered will be a measure of how often this code runs.

The primary advantage of a sampling profiler is that it can run without modifying the source program, and thus has very little overhead. The program runs at almost full speed when being profiled. The downside of the profiler is that the data is statistical in nature, and may not reflect exactly how the program executed. However, when sampled over a reasonable period of time (say a few hundred milliseconds at least), the results are accurate enough to form a good understanding of how the program performs, and what its bottlenecks are.

Using the profiler

The profiler lives within the *Profile* standard library package. So the first step in using the profiler is to import its namespace into the current session. You can do this using the `using` command:

```
julia> using Profile
```

This makes the `@profile` macro available. This measures and stores the performance profile of the expression supplied to it.

Do not profile the JIT:

As with measuring the time of execution, remember to run your code at least once before attempting to profile it. Otherwise, you will end up profiling the Julia JIT compiler, rather than your code. If you see many instances of `inference.jl` in your profiler output, that means you are profiling the compiler instead of your code. If you see this, clear the profile data, and run your code again; on the second run, you will get the correct profile results.

To see how the profiler works, let's start with a function that creates 1,000 sets of 10,000 random numbers, and then computes the mean of the squares for each set:

```
using Statistics
function randmsq()
    x = rand(10000, 1000)
    y = mean(x.^2, dims=1)
    return y
end
```

After calling the function once to ensure that all the code is compiled, we can run the profiler over this code as follows:

```
julia> randmsq();

julia> @profile randmsq()
```

This will execute the function while collecting profile information. The function will return as normal, and the collected profile information will be stored in memory.

The output from the profiler is a hierarchical list of code locations, representing the call stack for the program. The number, against each line, counts the number of times this line was sampled by the profiler. Therefore, the higher the number, the greater the contribution of that line to the total runtime of the program. It indicates the time spent on the line, and all its *callees*. If the hierarchy is too deeply nested, thereby making the output confusing, you can get a flat output by calling `Profile.print(format=:flat)`.

The profile information can be printed via the `print` method as follows:

```
julia> Profile.print()
115 ./task.jl:257; (::getfield(REPL,
Symbol("##28#29")){REPL.REPLBackend})()
 115 ...r/share/julia/stdlib/v0.7/REPL/src/REPL.jl:116; macro expansion
  115 ...r/share/julia/stdlib/v0.7/REPL/src/REPL.jl:85;
eval_user_input(::Any, ::REPL.REPLBackend)
   115 ./boot.jl:316; eval(::Module, ::Any)
    115 ./<missing>:0; top-level scope
     115 .../julia/stdlib/v0.7/Profile/src/Profile.jl:27; macro expansion
      53 ./REPL[11]:2; randmsq()
       53 ...e/julia/stdlib/v0.7/Random/src/Random.jl:224; rand
        53 .../julia/stdlib/v0.7/Random/src/Random.jl:236; rand
         53 .../julia/stdlib/v0.7/Random/src/Random.jl:235; rand
          8 ./boot.jl:407; Type
           8 ./boot.jl:400; Type
            8 ./boot.jl:392; Type
          45 .../julia/stdlib/v0.7/Random/src/Random.jl:214; rand!
           45 ...e/julia/stdlib/v0.7/Random/src/RNGs.jl:447; rand!

. . .
```

What does this output tell us? Well, among other things, it shows that the creation of the random arrays took a majority of the execution time; over a third. Of the remaining time, the majority was spent on the squaring, and a minority on the mean.

There are a few options to the profiler that are sometimes useful, although the defaults are a good choice for most uses. Primary among them is the *sampling interval*. This can be provided as keyword arguments to the `Profile.init()` method. The default delay is 1 millisecond on Linux, and should be increased for very long-running programs through a line of code such as the following (which sets the delay to 100 ms):

```
julia> Profile.init(delay=.01)
```

The delay may be reduced as well, but the overhead of profiling can increase significantly if it is lowered too much.

Finally, you may have realized that the profiler stores its samples in memory in order to be viewed later. In order to profile a different program during a Julia session that is already running, it may be necessary to clear the stored profile from memory. The `Profile.clear()` function does this, and must therefore be run between any two invocations of `@profile` within the same Julia process.

ProfileView

The textual display of the profiler output shown previously is useful and explanatory in many cases, but can become confusing to read for long, or deeply nested call graphs. In this case, or in general, if you prefer a graphical output, the `ProfileView` package is the answer. However, this is not included in the base Julia distribution, and must be installed as an external package via the Julia package manager:

```
julia> using Pkg

julia> Pkg.add("ProfileView")
```

This will install the `ProfileView` package and its dependencies (which include the Gtk graphical environment). Once installed, it is very simple to use. Simply load the package and call its `view()` function instead of `Profile.print()` after the profile samples have been collected using `@profile`:

```
julia> using ProfileView

julia> ProfileView.view()
```

A user interface window will pop up, with the profile displayed as a *flame graph*, similar to the following screenshot. Move your cursor over the blocks to note a hover containing the details of the call location:

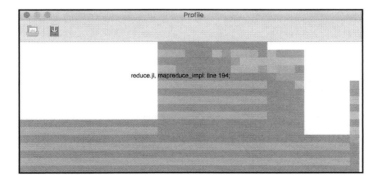

This view provides the same information as the tree view seen earlier, but may be easier to navigate and understand, particularly for larger programs. In this chart, elapsed time goes from left to right, while the call stack goes from bottom to top. The width of the bar therefore shows the time spent by the program in a particular call location, along with its callees. The bars stacked on top of one another show the hierarchy of function calls. This view of a program's execution profile is commonly known as a **flame graph**.

The `ProfileView` UI provides a few nifty utilities to work with the profile data. The profile itself can be saved to disk using the save icon at the top of the window, while a previously saved profile can be opened by clicking the folder icon. Right-clicking on a bar will cause an editor to open the program at that line, and left-clicking will cause a line describing the call to be printed in the Julia REPL. The latter is an easy way to quickly mark interesting lines, for subsequent analysis.

`ProfileView` also has the ability to create the flame graph in SVG format, which makes it easy to share profiling results with others. SVG is also the default format when `ProfileView` is called from within an IJulia notebook:

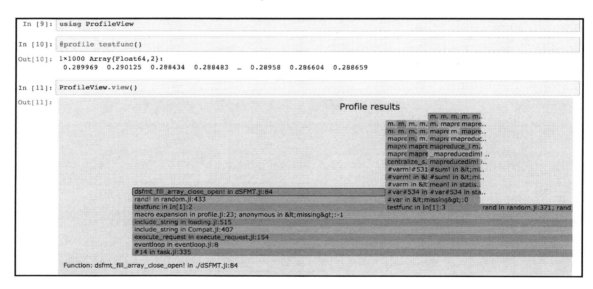

From the REPL, the `svgwrite` function can be used to output the graph in SVG format.

```
julia> ProfileView.svgwrite("profile_results.svg")
```

Using the profiler on the Julia REPL is simple, as we saw in this section, but it is also possible to use it in an integrated manner within an IDE.

Using Juno for profiling

The Juno IDE is a popular environment for developing Julia code. It is bundled with JuliaPro, and can also be installed directly. Among its many productivity enhancing features (such as inline evaluation, code completion, and a built-in debugger) is an integrated profiler. This provides a display of the profiler output on top of the source code view, making it easy to visualize the relative contribution of each line of code to the overall execution time.

While the display is more sophisticated, using the profiler in Juno is similar: use the @profiler macro (note the extra *r* at the end). The following screenshot shows an example of the profiler view inside Juno:

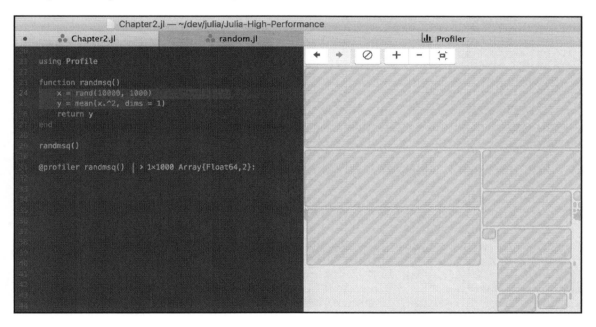

You will notice the highlight on top of the source code of the function being analyzed, depicting the performance cost of each line as an inline bar. On the right, there is a more traditional flame graph. Hovering on the boxes in the flame graph displays the file and function that it denotes, and clicking on the box will open the relevant source code in the IDE.

Using TimerOutputs

For some complicated and long-running programs, a full profiler run can be complex and confusing. Scrolling through many hundreds of stack frames becomes tedious. In these situations, the TimerOutput package helps to easily measure the constituent parts of a program.

To use this package, first install it using Julia's package manager:

```
julia> using Pkg
julia> Pkg.add("TimerOutputs");
```

Once installed, the package can be loaded. Next, a global TimerOutput object is created. This will store the results of our timing runs:

```
julia> using TimerOutputs

julia> const to = TimerOutput();
```

Now, we can time individual parts of the computation. We will reuse the randmsq function we wrote previously. We annotate the code inside the function via the @timeit macro, which takes as an argument the TimerOutput object, a name to refer to each invocation, and the expression to be measured:

```
function randmsq_timed()
    @timeit to "randmsq" begin
        x = @timeit to "rand" rand(10000, 1000)
        y = @timeit to "mean" mean(x.^2, dims=1)
        return y
    end
end
```

We now run this function, and then view the timer outputs using the `print_time` function:

```julia
julia> randmsq_timed();

julia> print_timer(to)
```

		Time			Allocations		
Tot / % measured:		53.0s / 0.83%			173MiB / 88.3%		
Section	ncalls	time	%tot	avg	alloc	%tot	avg
randmsq	2	438ms	100%	219ms	153MiB	100%	76.3MiB
rand	1	250ms	57.0%	250ms	76.3MiB	50.0%	76.3MiB
mean	1	188ms	43.0%	188ms	76.3MiB	50.0%	76.3MiB

The output nicely summarizes the timings for the nested calls, and calculates the aggregates. For long simulations, or complex optimization problems, this way of measuring timings can be very useful.

Analyzing memory allocation

The amount of memory used by a program is sometimes as important to track as the amount of time taken to run it. This is not only because memory is a limited resource that can be in short supply, but also because excessive allocation can easily lead to excessive execution time. The time taken to allocate and deallocate memory and run the garbage collection can become quite significant when a program uses large amounts of memory.

The `@time` macro seen in the previous sections provides information about memory allocation for the expression or function being timed. In some cases, however, it may be difficult to predict where exactly the memory allocation occurs. For these situations, Julia's track allocation functionality is just what is needed.

Using the memory allocation tracker

To get Julia to track memory allocation, start the `julia` process from your command or shell prompt with the `-track-allocation=user` option as follows:

```
$ julia track-allocation=user
```

This will start a normal Julia session in which you can run your code as usual. However, in the background, Julia will track all the memory used, which will be written to `.mem` files when Julia exits. There will be a new `.mem` file for each `.jl` file that is loaded and executed. These files will contain the Julia code from their corresponding source files, with each line annotated with the total amount of memory that was allocated as a result of executing this line.

As we discussed earlier, when running Julia code, the compiler will compile the user code at runtime. Once again, we do not want to measure the memory allocation due to the compiler. To achieve this, first run the code under measurement once, after starting the Julia process. Then, run the `Profile.clear_malloc_data()` function to restart the allocation measurement counters. Finally, run the code under measurement once again, and then exit the process. This way, we will get the most accurate memory measurements.

Statistically accurate benchmarking

The tools described in this chapter, particularly the `@time` macro, are useful for identifying and investigating bottlenecks in our program. However, they are not very accurate in terms of a fine-grained analysis of fast programs. If you want to, for example, compare two functions that take a few milliseconds to run, the amount of error and variability in the measurement will easily swamp the running time of this function.

Using BenchmarkTools.jl

The solution, then, is to use the `BenchmarkTools.jl` package for statistically accurate benchmarking. Install the package via the Julia package manager, and thereafter it is simple to use. Instead of using `@time`, use the `@benchmark` macro. Unlike `@time`, however, this macro can only be used in front of function calls, rather than any expression. It will evaluate the parameters of the function separately, and then call the function multiple times to build up a sample of execution times.

The output will show the mean time taken to run the code, but with statistically accurate upper and lower bounds. These statistics are estimated by evaluating the expression multiple times, with the number of evaluations determined in order to maximize the accuracy of the measurements. These estimates attempt to account for the noise inherent in running benchmarks on real machines, while also minimizing the time taken to measure it accurately. As an example, we measure the running time of creating a random array and calculating the square root of all its elements:

```
julia> using BenchmarkTools

julia> @benchmark sqrt.(rand(1000))
BenchmarkTools.Trial:
  memory estimate: 15.88 KiB
  allocs estimate: 2
  --------------
  minimum time: 6.266 μs (0.00% GC)
  median time: 7.225 μs (0.00% GC)
  mean time: 9.417 μs (13.12% GC)
  maximum time: 612.404 μs (96.45% GC)
  --------------
  samples: 10000
  evals/sample: 5
```

A simpler version of the output can be obtained by using the @btime macro. This macro does the same operations as the @benchmark macro, but provides simpler output that is similar to the basic @time macro. Furthermore, it also returns the value of the expression that it evaluated. For the rest of the book, this is what we will use for all time measurements for the code that we write and evaluate. Using the @btime macro from the BenchmarkTools package will allow us to be confident that any performance improvements to our code that we measure are real, and not noise:

```
julia> @btime mean(rand(1000));
  1.665 μs (1 allocation: 7.94 KiB)e
```

 The BenchmarkTools package consists of sophisticated machinery to provide statistically accurate benchmarking. The theory behind the code is explained in Jarett Ravel and Jiahao Chen's paper, *Robust benchmarking in noisy environments*, available at https://arxiv.org/abs/1608.04295.

These two macros, @benchmark and @btime, should be your standard method to measure performance in Julia. They should be used in almost all cases in which you need to benchmark any code. We will use them almost exclusively throughout this book. All the code in subsequent chapters will assume that the package has been loaded in the session by using BenchmarkTools. In rare cases, such as for long-running programs that take too long and cannot be executed multiple times, you may fall back to the @time macro. However, such occasions should be rare.

Summary

In this chapter, we discussed how to use the available tools to measure the performance of Julia code. We learned to measure the time and memory resources used by code, and understood how to arrive at the hotspots for any program.

In subsequent chapters, we will learn how to remedy the issues we encounter using the tools of this chapter, and hence improve the performance measurements for our code.

Types, Type Inference, and Stability

3

Julia is a dynamically typed language. Unlike languages such as Java or C, the programmer does not need to specify the fixed type of every variable in the program. Yet, somewhat counterintuitively, Julia achieves its impressive performance characteristics by inferring and using the type information for all the data in the program. In this chapter, we will start with a brief look at the type system in the language and then explain how to use this type system to write high-performance code.

This chapter will cover the following topics:

- The Julia type system
- Type inference
- Type stability
- Types at storage locations

The Julia type system

Types in Julia are essentially tags, on values, that restrict the range of potential values that can possibly be stored at that location. Being a dynamic language, these tags are relevant only to runtime values. Types are usually not enforced at compile time; rather, they are checked at runtime. However, type information is used at compile time to generate specialized methods for different kinds of function arguments.

Using types

In most dynamic languages, types are implicit in terms of how values are created. Julia can be—and usually is—written in this way, with no explicit type annotations. However, optionally, you can indicate variables or function parameters to be restricted to specific types using the :: symbol. Here are a few examples.

We define two versions of the iam function, one for integer arguments and another for string arguments. We also define a single method for the function addme, which takes two unrestricted values of any kind as an argument, as follows:

```
#Declare type of function argument
iam(x::Integer) = "an integer"
iam(x::String) = "a string"

function addme(a, b)
  #Declare type of local variable x
  x::Int64 = 2
  #Type of variable y will be inferred
  y = (a+b) / x
  return y
end
```

Having defined these functions, we can now call them. These calls should make clear how Julia dispatches function calls based on the types of the argument values, as follows:

```
julia> iam(1)                              #Dispatch on type of
argument
"an integer"

julia> iam("1")                            #Dispatch on type of
argument
"a string"

julia> iam(1.5)                            #Dispatch fails
ERROR: `iam` has no method matching iam(::Float64)
```

A note on terminology

In Julia, the abstract operation represented by a name is called a function, while the individual implementations for specific types are called methods. Thus, in the preceding code, we can use the iam function and the iam methods for Integer and String. In an object-oriented language, objects have methods; in Julia, functions have methods.

Multiple dispatch

If there were one unifying strand throughout the design of the Julia language, it would be **multiple dispatch**. Simply put, dispatch is the process of selecting a function to be executed at runtime. Multiple dispatch, then, is the method of determining the function to be called based on the types of the parameters of the function. Thus, one of the most important uses of types in Julia programs is to arrange the appropriate method dispatch by specifying the types of function arguments.

 Note that this is different from the concept of method overloading. Method overloading happens on types known at compile time, while dispatch happens on the actual types of values at runtime.

Dispatch is a runtime process, while method overloading is a compile-time concept. In most traditional object-oriented languages, dispatch at runtime occurs only on the runtime type of the **receiver** of the method (for example, the object before the dot), hence the term **single dispatch**.

Julia programs, therefore, usually contain many small method definitions for different types of arguments. It is good practice, however, to constrain argument types to the widest level possible. Use tight constraints only when you know that the method will fail on other types. Otherwise, write your method to accept unconstrained types and depend on the runtime to dispatch nested calls to the correct methods.

As an example, consider the following function to compute the sum of the square of two numbers:

```
sumsqr(x, y) = x^2 + y^2
```

In this code, we do not specify any type constrains for the x and y arguments of our sumsqr function. The base library will contain different + and ^ methods for integers and floats, and the runtime will dispatch to the correct method based on the types of the arguments.

In the following code, we call the `sumsqr` function with integers, floats, complex numbers, and a combination of these:

```julia
julia> sumsqr(1, 2)
5

julia> sumsqr(1.5, 2.5)
8.5

julia> sumsqr(1 + 2im , 2 + 3im)
-8 + 16im


julia> sumsqr(2 + 2im, 2.5)
6.25 + 8.0im
```

The use of multiple dispatches is thus at the heart of implementation and design for all Julia code.

Abstract types

Types in Julia can be concrete or abstract. Abstract types cannot have any instantiated values. In other words, they can only be the nodes of the type hierarchy, not its leaves. They also do not have any fields, and thus cannot hold any data. They represent sets of related types. For example, Julia contains integer types for 32-bit and 64-bit integers, `Int32` and `Int64` respectively. Both these types inherit from the `Signed` abstract type, which in turn inherits from the `Integer` abstract type.

Abstract types are defined using the `abstract type` keyword. The inheritance relationship between types is denoted using the `<:` symbol followed by the name of the parent (super) type. As an example, shown here are some of the abstract types defined as the basis of Julia's number system:

```julia
abstract type Number ; end
abstract type Real      <: Number  ; end
abstract type FloatingPoint <: Real   ; end
abstract type Integer   <: Real  ; end
abstract type Signed    <: Integer  ; end
abstract type Unsigned <: Integer ; end
```

You will notice that the `Number` type is declared without any explicit super type. It is implicitly the direct subtype of the type at the top of the hierarchy in Julia—the `Any` type. We will talk more about this hierarchy in the next section.

Concrete types, on the other hand, are the types that can be instantiated to values. Thus, every value in Julia is of one concrete type. One of the most important points to note about concrete types is that they cannot have any subtypes. Only abstract types can be subtyped. In other words, all concrete types are declared *final* in Julia.

Julia's type hierarchy

All types in Julia live within a type hierarchy. This hierarchy is rooted at the top by the `Any` type. All Julia types, without exception, live within this hierarchy. In particular, unlike languages such as Java, there is no distinction between so-called primitive types and reference types. While there may be differences as to how the numbers are represented internally compared to user-defined types, as far as the type system is concerned, they form a unified hierarchy.

When a type declaration is omitted for a variable or parameter (as in many of the examples in the previous chapter), it can contain values of any type. This is denoted by the special `Any` type. The `Any` type can therefore be seen as being at the top of Julia's type hierarchy. All other Julia types are subtypes of this type. Visualizing the type hierarchy of some of the numeric types, described in the `Chapter 1`, *Julia is Fast*, is instructive:

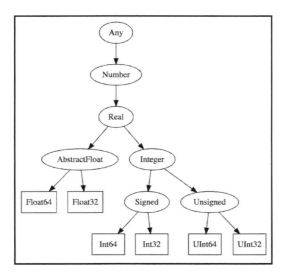

At the other end of the spectrum resides the `Union{}` type. This type lives at the bottom of the type hierarchy. All types are super types of `Union{}`, and there can be no actual instances of this type.

Another common type is the `Nothing` type. This type has a single instance defined, named `nothing`. This is typically used to denote the absence of a value. For example, methods that don't return any other value return `nothing`. It is also used when you need a `void` value in calls to C libraries.

Composite and immutable types

Composite types in Julia are collections of named fields. They are equivalent to a `struct` in C and can be thought of as roughly equivalent to a class without behavior (or a data class) in object-oriented languages. They are defined with the `struct` keyword and contain the names and types of the fields within them.

Take a look at the following code, which defines the `Pixel` type and can be used to store a position and color for a single pixel on screen:

```
struct Pixel
    x::Int64
    y::Int64
    color::Int64
end

julia> p = Pixel(5,5, 100)
Pixel(5,5,100)

julia> p.x = 10;
ERROR: type Pixel is immutable

julia> p.x
5
```

Types created with the `struct` keyword are *immutable* by default, which means that the values of its fields cannot be changed after an instance is created. In cases where this is undesirable, a *mutable* type can be declared using the `mutable struct` keyword. In this case, the fields values can be changed at any time. Take a look at the following code:

```
mutable struct MPixel
    x::Int64
    y::Int64
    color::Int64
end

julia> p = MPixel(5,5, 100)
MPixel(5,5,100)
```

```
julia> p.x=10;

julia> p.x
10


julia> @show p
p = MPixel(10, 5, 100)
```

In the next section, we will enhance composite types by adding type parameters.

Type parameters

Type parameters are one of the most useful and powerful features of Julia's type system. This is the ability to use parameters when defining types (or functions), thereby defining a whole set of types, one for each value of the parameter. This is analogous to generic or template programming in other languages.

Type parameters are declared within curly braces. For the preceding `Pixel` type, if we wanted to store `color` as either an integer, a hexadecimal string, or as an structured RGB type, we would define its type to be parameterized. In this case, the unadorned name, `Pixel`, becomes an abstract type, and `Pixel{Int64}` or `Pixel{String}` are the concrete subtypes of `Pixel`:

```
struct Pixel{T}
    x::Int64
    y::Int64
    color::T
end
```

Parameters of a type are usually other types. This will be familiar if you have used template classes in C++ or Java generics. In Julia, however, type parameters are not always restricted to be other types. They can be values, though they are restricted to a set of constant, immutable types. Hence, you can use, among others, integer or symbol values as type parameters.

The built-in `Array{T, N}` type is a good example of this usage. This type is parameterized by two parameters, one of which is a type, and the other is a value. The first parameter, `T`, is the type of elements in the array. The second, `N`, is an integer specifying the number of dimensions in the array.

The addition of type parameters provides more information to the compiler about the composition of the values in memory. For example, it allows the programmer to assert—or the compiler to infer—the types of elements stored within a container. This, as we'll discuss in the next section, allows the compiler to generate code that is, in turn, optimized to the types and storage method in question.

Type inference

Types in Julia are optional and unobtrusive. The type system usually keeps out of the way of the programmer. It is not necessary or recommended to annotate all the variables with type information.

This is not to say that type information is redundant. Quite the opposite is true, in fact. A large part of Julia's speed comes from the ability of the compiler to compile and cache specialized versions of each function for all the possible types to which it can be applied. This means that most functions can be compiled down to their best possible optimized representations.

To achieve this balance, the runtime tries to figure out as much type information as it can through type inference. The algorithm is based on forward dataflow analysis. It should be noted that this is not an implementation of the famous Hindley-Milner algorithm using unification, which is used in the **Meta Language** (**ML**) family of languages, such as OCaml and F#. In these languages, it is mandatory for the compiler to be able to determine the type of every value in the system. In Julia, however, type inference can be performed on a best-effort basis, with any failure handled with a runtime fallback.

As a simple example of visible type inference, consider the following line of code, which creates an array from a range of integers. This code does not have any type annotations, yet the runtime is able to create an array with properly typed elements of Int64:

```
julia>[x for x in 1:5]
5-element Array{Int64,1}:
 1
 2
 3
 4
 5
```

In this section, we provided a quick overview of some of the important features of types in Julia. For more information, visit the online documentation at https://docs.julialang.org/en/v1/manual/types/#man-types-1.

For the rest of this chapter, we will assume familiarity with these concepts and look at how they impact the performance of Julia code.

Type-stability

In order for the Julia compiler to compile a specialized version of a function for each different type of argument, it needs to infer, as best as possible, the parameter and return types of all functions. If it doesn't do this, the speed of Julia will be hugely compromised. In order to do this effectively, the code must be written in a way that it is type-stable.

Definitions

Type-stability is the idea that the type of the return value of a function is dependent only on the types of its arguments and not the values. When this is true, the compiler can infer the return type of a function by knowing the types of its inputs. This ensures that type inference can continue across chains of function invocations without actually running the code, even though the language is fully dynamic.

As an example, let's look at the following code, which returns the input for positive numbers but 0 for negative numbers:

```
function pos(x)
    if x < 0
        return 0
    else
        return x
    end
end
```

This code works for both integers and floating-point output, as follows:

```
julia> pos(-1)
0

julia> pos(-2.5)
0

julia> pos(2.5)
2.5
```

However, you may notice an issue with calling this function with the float input. Take a look at the following:

```
julia> typeof(pos(2.5))
Float64

julia> typeof(pos(-2.5))
Int64
```

The return type of the `pos` function in this case depends on the value of the input and not just its type. The type of the argument for both the preceding invocations is `Float64`. However, if the value of the input is less than zero, the type of the return is `Int64`. On the other hand, if the input value is zero or greater, then the type of output is `Float64`. This makes the function type-unstable.

Fixing type instability

Now that we can recognize type-unstable code, the question arises: how can we fix code such as this? There are two obvious solutions. One would be to write separate versions of the `pos` function for different input types. So, we could have a version of `pos` for integers and another for floating points. However, this would cause instances of repeated, copy-pasted code. Also, there would not just be two such instances; there would be copies for `Float32`, `Float64`, `Int32`, `Int64`, and so on. Further, we would have to write a new version of this function for all the new numeric types that were defined. It should be obvious that writing generic functions that operate on a wide variety of related types is really the best way to get concise and elegant Julia code.

The second obvious solution is to branch out the input type within the generic function. So, we could write code along these lines, as follows:

```
if typeof(x) == Float64
    return 0.0
elseif typeof(x) == Float32
    return Float32(0.0)
elseif typeof(x) == Int64
    return 0
......
end
```

I hope you can see that this can also quickly get tedious. However, this type of code provides us with a hint as to what the correct solution is. In Julia, whenever you find yourself explicitly checking the type of any variable, it is time to let dispatch do the job.

The Julia base library contains a `zero(x)` function that takes as its argument any numeric value and returns an appropriately typed zero value for this type. Using this function, let's implement the following polynomial. We do this in the `f_naive` function as follows:

```
function pos_fixed(x)
  if x < 0
    return zero(x)
  else
    return x
  end
end
```

The output of the code shows that the type instability is now fixed. An input of `Float64` always returns a value of type `Float64`, while an input of type `Int64` always returns an `Int64`:

```
julia> pos_fixed(-2.4)
0.0

julia> pos_fixed(-2)
0

julia> typeof(pos_fixed(-2.4))
Float64

julia> typeof(pos_fixed(-2))
Int64
```

In making the `pos` function type-stable, we used a standard library function to move the variable typed part of the code into another function. However, this principle applies even when you do not have a base function to fall back on—isolate the part of your function that varies depending on the type of the input and allow Julia's dispatch to call the correct piece of code depending on the type.

The performance pitfalls

Type stability has been historically very important for high-performance Julia code. In Julia 1.0, however, the compiler has improved significantly to the extent that simple instances of type instability can easily be optimized out, ensuring that simple type-unstable code is almost as fast as type-stable code. This is achieved via a compiler technique called **union splitting**.

Measuring the function runtimes in the following listing, we can see that the type-unstable version is only slightly slower than the type-stable one:

```
julia> @btime pos(2.5)
  0.032 ns (0 allocations: 0 bytes)
2.5


julia> @btime pos_fixed(2.5)
  0.031 ns (0 allocations: 0 bytes)
2.5
```

In older versions of Julia, this would have been half as fast as the type-stable version.

Does this mean that you should not worry about type stability any more? Well, no. As soon as things get more complicated, union splitting may fail. It is therefore important to understand and measure this phenomena. Many further optimizations the Julia compiler can do might be thwarted by the presence of type instability, even though a microbenchmark of a single function may not show that.

Thankfully, it is not that hard to identify type-unstable code. With the tools available within the language, you will be able to build up your intuition about this very quickly.

Identifying type stability

In the preceding `pos` function, the type instability was found by reading and understanding the code. In many cases where the code is longer or more complicated, it may not be easy or even possible to understand the type behavior of a function merely by inspection. It would be useful to have some tools at our disposal.

Fortunately, Julia provides the `@code_warntype` macro, which enables us to view the types inferred by the compiler, thereby identifying any type instability in our code. The output of `@code_warntype` is the lowered, type-inferred **abstract syntax tree (AST)** structure. In other words, the compiler parses and processes the source code into a standardized form and then runs the type inference on the result to figure out the possible types of all the variables and function calls within the code.

Let's run this on our type-unstable method and take a look at what it says, as follows:

```
julia> @code_warntype pos(2.5)
Body::Union{Float64, Int64}
1 ─ %1 = (Base.lt_float)(x, 0.0)::Bool
  │ %2 = (Base.eq_float)(x, 0.0)::Bool
  │ %3 = (Base.and_int)(%2, true)::Bool
  │ %4 = (Base.and_int)(%3, false)::Bool
  │ %5 = (Base.or_int)(%1, %4)::Bool
  └     goto #3 if not %5
2 ─     return 0
3 ─     return x
```

While this output might look slightly scary at first, the relevant portions are easy to highlight. If you run this on Julia's REPL, you will see that the first line of the output, `Union{Float64, Int64}`, is highlighted in red. This line shows that the compiler inferred that the return type of this function, when passed `Float64` as an argument, can either be `Float64` or `Int64`. Therefore, this function is type-unstable, and this is made obvious by the red highlight in the REPL.

In general, the output from `@code_warntype`, as the name suggests, will warn us of any type-inference problem in the code, highlighting it in red. These will usually be variables for which the compiler cannot infer any bound, shown as `Any`, or where there are multiple options for possible types, shown as `Union`. While there are some cases where these warnings might be false positives, they should always be investigated if they are unexpected.

If we run this macro on the `pos_fixed` function, which we made type-stable, we will see that the compiler can infer `Float64` as the return type of the function. Upon running this on the REPL, there is no red font in the output, giving us confidence that the function is type-stable. Take a look at the following:

```
[julia> @code_warntype pos_fixed(2.5)
Body::Float64
1 ─ %1 = (Base.lt_float)(x, 0.0)::Bool
│     %2 = (Base.eq_float)(x, 0.0)::Bool
│     %3 = (Base.and_int)(%2, true)::Bool
│     %4 = (Base.and_int)(%3, false)::Bool
│     %5 = (Base.or_int)(%1, %4)::Bool
└──        goto #3 if not %5
2 ─        return 0.0
3 ─        return x
```

Further evidence of the benefits of type-stability can be observed by looking at the LLVM bitcode produced by the Julia compiler. This can be seen using the `@code_llvm` macro, which outputs the result of compiling the Julia code into LLVM bitcode:

```
julia> @code_llvm pos(2.5)

define { %jl_value_t addrspace(10)*, i8 } @julia_pos_35641([8 x i8]*
noalias nocapture align 8 dereferenceable(8), double) {
top:
  %2 = fcmp uge double %1, 0.000000e+00
  br i1 %2, label %L10, label %L9

L9: ; preds = %L10, %top
  %merge = phi { %jl_value_t addrspace(10)*, i8 } [ { %jl_value_t
addrspace(10)* addrspacecast (%jl_value_t* inttoptr (i64 4523720160 to
%jl_value_t*) to %jl_value_t addrspace(10)*), i8 -126 }, %top ], [ {
%jl_value_t addrspace(10)* addrspacecast (%jl_value_t* null to %jl_value_t
addrspace(10)*), i8 1 }, %L10 ]
  ret { %jl_value_t addrspace(10)*, i8 } %merge

L10: ; preds = %top
  %.0..sroa_cast = bitcast [8 x i8]* %0 to double*
  store double %1, double* %.0..sroa_cast, align 8
  br label %L9
}
```

When we see the output of the same macro on the fixed code, it should be obvious that the type-stable function compiles a much smaller amount of code, even if the details of the output are not very understandable. It comprises fewer instructions and that, to a certain extent, corresponds with faster code:

```
julia> @code_llvm pos_fixed(2.5)
define double @julia_pos_fixed_35642(double) {
top:
  %.inv = fcmp olt double %0, 0.000000e+00
  %spec.select = select i1 %.inv, double 0.000000e+00, double %0
  ret double %spec.select
}
```

If you are more comfortable with assembly instructions than with LLVM bitcode, the same inference can be gleaned from looking at the final assembly instructions that the Julia code compiles to. This can be output using the @code_native macro and is the final code that gets run on the computer's processor:

```
julia> @code_native pos(2.5)
  vxorps %xmm1, %xmm1, %xmm1
  vucomisd %xmm0, %xmm1
  ja L19
  vmovsd %xmm0, (%edi)
  movb $1, %dl
  xorl %eax, %eax
  retl
L19:
  movb $-126, %dl
  decl %eax
  movl $228752864, %eax ## imm = 0xDA27DE0
  addl %eax, (%eax)
  addb %al, (%eax)
  retl

julia> @code_native pos_fixed(2.5)
  vxorpd %xmm1, %xmm1, %xmm1
  vmaxsd %xmm0, %xmm1, %xmm0
  retl
  nopl (%eax)
;}
```

This output is the result of the full gamut of compiler optimizations implemented by the Julia compiler, as well as LLVM's **Just In Time** (**JIT**) compiler. Looking at the output for our usual functions, we can see once again that the type-stable function does significantly less work, as follows:

```
julia> @code_native pos_fixed(2.5)
  vxorpd %xmm1, %xmm1, %xmm1
  vmaxsd %xmm0, %xmm1, %xmm0
  retl
  nopl (%eax)
```

Loop variables

Another facet of type-stability that is important in Julia is that variables within a loop should not change their type from one iteration of the loop to another. Let's first look at a case where this is not true, as follows:

```
function sumsqrtn(n)
    r = 0
    for i = 1:n
        r = r + sqrt(i)
    end
    return r
end
```

In this function, the r variable starts out as Int64, when the loop is entered in the first iteration. However, the sqrt function returns Float64, which, when added to Int64, returns Float64. At this point, at line four of the function, r becomes Float64. This violates the rule of not changing the type of variable within a loop and makes this code type-unstable.

Inspecting the @code_warntype output for this function makes this obvious. Viewing this in the REPL, we're faced with types of variables printed in red, which are highlighted in bold in the listing that follows:

```
julia> @code_warntype sumsqrtn(5)
Body::Union{Float64, Int64}
1 ── %1 = (Base.sle_int)(1, n)::Bool
│    %2 = (Base.ifelse)(%1, n, 0)::Int64
│    %3 = (Base.slt_int)(%2, 1)::Bool
└───      goto #3 if not %3
2 ──      goto #4
3 ──      goto #4
4 ── %7 = φ (#2 => true, #3 => false)::Bool
│    %8 = φ (#3 => 1)::Int64
```

```
|     %9 = φ (#3 => 1)::Int64
|     %10 = (Base.not_int)(%7)::Bool
└────── goto #19 if not %10
5 ──── %12 = φ (#4 => 0, #18 => %36)::Union{Float64, Int64}
...
...
17 ── %42 = φ (#16 => %40)::Int64
|     %43 = φ (#16 => %40)::Int64
|     %44 = φ (#15 => true, #16 => false)::Bool
|     %45 = (Base.not_int)(%44)::Bool
└────── goto #19 if not %45
18 ── goto #5
19 ── %48 = φ (#17 => %36, #4 => 0)::Union{Float64, Int64}
└────── return %48
```

This output shows that the function itself can return either Float64 or Int64 (it is typed as Union{Float64,Int64}).

Fixing the instability is easy in this case. We just need to initialize the r variable to be the Float64 value, as we know that is the type it will eventually take. Take a look at the following function now:

```
function sumsqrtn_fixed(n)
    r = 0.0
    for i = 1:n
        r = r + sqrt(i)
    end
    return r
end
```

The @code_warntype output for this function is now clean, with the return value inferred as Float64 in the output:

```
julia> @code_warntype sumsqrtn_fixed(5)
Body::Float64
1 ──── %1 = (Base.sle_int)(1, n)::Bool
|     %2 = (Base.ifelse)(%1, n, 0)::Int64
|     %3 = (Base.slt_int)(%2, 1)::Bool
└────── goto #3 if not %3
...
...
13 ── goto #5
14 ── %35 = φ (#12 => %23, #4 => 0.0)::Float64
└────── return %35
```

While we've truncated the output in the preceding listing, when you run this yourself you will notice that the generated code for the type stable code is much smaller.

Once again, the latest Julia versions can optimize much of this away, with the difference in performance being much less than it used to be:

```
julia> @btime sumsqrtn(1000_000)
  4.866 ms (0 allocations: 0 bytes)
6.666671664588418e8

julia> @btime sumsqrtn_fixed(1000_000)
  4.828 ms (0 allocations: 0 bytes)
6.666671664588418e8
```

However, it is still worthwhile to watch out for these issues. Doing so will generate much cleaner machine code, which will guarantee high performance without any surprises. As an example, consider the following code. This is very similar to the previous code examples, but with **SIMD** annotations added:

```
function simdsum(x)
    s = 0
    @simd for v in x
        s += v
    end
    return s
end

function simdsum_fixed(x)
    s = zero(eltype(x))
    @simd for v in A
        s += v
    end
    return s
end
```

If we benchmark this code, we will find that the type-stable code is over five times faster:

```
julia> a = rand(Float32, 10^6);

julia> @btime simdsum(a)
  1.052 ms (0 allocations: 0 bytes)
499576.7f0

julia> @btime simdsum_fixed(a)
  191.393 μs (0 allocations: 0 bytes)
499571.12f0
```

Type stability thus remains a very important consideration for creating high-performance Julia code.

Kernel methods and function barriers

Type inference in Julia primarily works by inspecting the types of function parameters and identifying the type of the return value. This suggests that some type instability issues may be mitigated by breaking up a function into smaller functions. This can provide additional hints to the compiler, making more accurate type inferencing possible.

For an example of this, consider a contrived function that takes as input the string `"Int64"` or `"Float64"` and returns an array of 10 elements, the types of which correspond to the type name passed as the input argument. Functions such as this may arise when creating arrays based on user input or by reading a file in which the type of the output is determined at runtime. Take a look at the following:

```julia
function string_zeros(s::AbstractString)
    n=1000_000
    x = s=="Int64" ?
        Vector{Int64}(undef,n)  :
        Vector{Float64}(undef, n)
    for i in 1:length(x)
        x[i] = 0
    end
    return x
end
```

We will benchmark this code to find an average execution time of over 28 milliseconds per function call with a large memory allocation, as shown in the following code:

```julia
julia> @btime string_zeros("Int64");
  28.465 ms (999491 allocations: 22.88 MiB)
```

This seems to be unnecessarily high. The loop in the function is the obvious place where most of the time is spent within this function. We note that in this loop, the type of the variable being accessed, x, cannot be known before the function is called, even when the type of the function arguments is known. This prevents the compiler from generating an optimized loop operating on one specific type.

What we need to do is ensure that the loop operates in a way so that the type of the x variable is known to the compiler. As we said earlier, type inference operates on function boundaries, which suggests a solution to our conundrum. We can split out the loop into its own function, separating the determination of the type of x and the operations on x across a function call, as follows:

```julia
function string_zeros_stable(s::AbstractString)
    n = 1000_000
    x = s=="Int64" ?
```

```
            Vector{Int64}(undef, n) :
            Vector{Float64}(undef, n)
        return fill_zeros(x)
    end

    function fill_zeros(x)
        for i in 1:length(x)
            x[i] = 0
        end
        return x
    end
```

Now, by benchmarking this solution, we will find that the execution time of our function reduces enormously, with a significant fall in the allocated memory:

```
julia> @btime string_zeros_stable("Int64");
 1.094 ms (2 allocations: 7.63 MiB)
```

Therefore, in situations where the types of variables are uncertain, we need to be careful in ensuring that the compiler is provided as much information as necessary.

Types in storage locations

We discussed in the earlier sections that when writing idiomatic Julia code, we should try and write functions with the minimum amount of type constraints possible in order to write generic code. We do not need to specify the types of function arguments or local variables for performance reasons. The compiler will be able to infer the required types. Thus, while the types are important, they are usually optional when writing Julia code. In general, bindings do not need to be typed; they are inferred.

However, when defining storage locations for data, it is important to specify a concrete type. So, for things that hold data, such as arrays, dictionaries, or fields in composite types, it is best to explicitly define the type that it will hold.

Arrays

As an example, let's create two arrays containing the same data: the numbers one to ten, which are of the Int64 type. The first array we will create is defined to hold values of the Int64 type. The second is defined to hold values of the abstract Number type, which is a supertype of Int64.

Take a look at the following code:

```
julia> a = Int64[1, 2, 3, 4, 5, 6, 7, 8, 9, 10]
10-element Array{Int64,1}:
   1
   2
 ...
   9
  10

julia> b = Number[1,2,3,4,5,6,7,8,9,10]
10-element Array{Number,1}:
   1
   2
 ...
   9
  10
```

We will then pass these arrays into the following function, which calculates the sum of squares of the elements of these arrays:

```
function arr_sumsqr(x::Array{T}) where T <: Number
    r = zero(T)
    for i = 1:length(x)
        r = r + x[i] ^ 2
    end
    return r
end
```

By timing the invocations, we will see that when using the Int64 array, this computation is over 30 times faster than when using the Number array, even when the data within the arrays themselves are identical:

```
julia> @btime arr_sumsqr($a)
  9.691 ns (0 allocations: 0 bytes)
385

julia> @btime arr_sumsqr($b)
  379.391 ns (0 allocations: 0 bytes)
385
```

The reason for this massive difference lies in how the values are stored within the array. When the array is defined to contain a specific concrete type, the Julia runtime can store the values inline within the allocation of the array, since it knows the exact size of each element. When the array contains an abstract type, the actual value can be of any size. Thus, when the Julia runtime creates the array, it only stores the pointers to the actual values within the array. The values are stored elsewhere on the heap. This not only causes extra memory load when reading the values, but the indirection can mess up pipelining and cache affinity when executing this code on the CPU.

Composite types

There is another situation where concrete types must be specified for good performance, which is done in the fields of composite types.

As an example, consider a composite type for holding the location of a point in 2D space. In this scenario, we could define the object as follows:

```
struct Point
    x
    y
end
```

However, this definition would perform quite badly. The primary issue is that the x and y fields in this type can be used to store values of any type. In particular, they could be other complex structs accessed as pointers. In this case, the compiler will not know whether access to the fields of the Point type requires a pointer indirection, and thus it cannot optimize the reading of these values.

It will be much better to define this type with the field values constrained to concrete types. This has two benefits. Firstly, the field values will be stored inline when the object is allocated rather than not being directed via pointer. Secondly, all code that uses fields of this type will be able to be type-inferred correctly. So, we define the type as follows:

```
struct ConcretePoint
    x::Float64
    y::Float64
end
```

Let's operate on these objects by writing a function that sums the elements of an array of `Points`:

```
function sumsqr_points(a)
    s=0.0
    for x in a
        s = s + x.x^2 + x.y^2
    end
    return s
end
```

```
julia> p_array = [Point(rand(), rand()) for i in 1:1000_000];

julia> cp_array = [ConcretePoint(rand(), rand()) for i in 1:1000_000];
```

Measuring the performance of this function, we see that using a concretely typed struct provides a performance boost of over 30 times in this case:

```
julia> @btime sumsqr_points($p_array)
  74.059 ms (3000000 allocations: 45.78 MiB)
667095.1292585902

julia> @btime sumsqr_points($cp_array)
  2.131 ms (1 allocation: 16 bytes)
666817.9767892341
```

Let's have a look at parametric composite types in the next section.

Parametric composite types

While the preceding definition of `ConcretePoint` performs well, it loses some significant flexibility. If we wanted to store the field values as `Float32` or `Float16`, we would be unable to use the same type. To lose so much flexibility for performance seems very unfortunate.

It would be tempting to fix this using an abstract type as the fields. In this case, all the concrete floating point numbers would be subtypes of the `AbstractFloat` type. We could then define a `PointsWithAbstract` type containing fields annotated as `AbstractFloat`, as follows:

```
struct PointWithAbstract
    x::AbstractFloat
    y::AbstractFloat
end
```

However, this code has the same drawbacks as the original `Point` type mentioned earlier. It will be slow, and the compiler will be unable to optimize the access to the type. The solution is to use a parametric type, as follows:

```
struct ParametricPoint{T <: AbstractFloat}
    x::T
    y::T
end
```

When we write the type in this manner, our code remains generic. We can write our methods knowing that the `ParametricPoint` type can hold values for any kind of a floating point number. Yet at runtime, when an instance of this type is created, it is instantiated with a particular type of float. In other words, once an instance is created, `T` becomes known. At this point, all the benefits of specifying the concrete type discussed before are applicable. Both storage and type inferences are efficient now. We can measure the performance to verify that having flexible types has not created any overhead in this case, as follows:

```
julia> pp_array = [ParametricPoint(rand(), rand()) for i in 1:1000_000];

julia> @btime sumsqr_points($pp_array)
 2.113 ms (1 allocation: 16 bytes)
666656.5530287792
```

Summary

In this chapter, we discussed how types play a crucial role in writing idiomatic and performant code in Julia. Much of what we discussed here is exactly what makes Julia a unique dynamic language where types, dispatch, and inference play a fundamental role.

We discussed how to write type-stable code, and when and how to define type annotations for performance. In the next chapter, we will discuss the performance characteristics of another important part of the language: functions.

4
Making Fast Function Calls

In Julia, the function is the primary unit of code structure. Idiomatic Julia code consists of many small functions that are defined with different types of arguments. In general, the overhead of a function call in Julia is very small, and, with type specialization, the compiled version of the function is very efficient. In this chapter, we will look at some of the techniques that Julia uses to make very fast function calls. We will also look at some limitations that are worth keeping in mind for the fastest code. Finally, we will look at some situations where moving code out of functions and into other structures, such as macros and staged functions, allows code to be faster and more efficient.

The following topics are covered in this chapter:

- Using globals
- Inlining
- Closures and anonymous functions
- Using macros for performance
- Using generated functions
- Using named parameters

Using globals

One of the first performance tips that you come across when learning Julia is the advice to not use global variables. This is usually not a very onerous requirement, as the global state is generally considered bad programming practice. Given how easy it is to fall into this trap and the large amount of performance degradation that can occur, it is important to keep this in mind when writing Julia code. This is particularly important when working on the REPL or in an IJulia notebook, since it is natural to create globals in those environments.

While we spend a lot of time in this chapter saying that globals are bad, they can often be very useful. After all, ease of use and programmer productivity is one of Julia's key features. So, our message is not "do not use globals." Rather, it is "do not use globals in performance critical parts of your code."

The trouble with globals

In the previous chapter, we saw how Julia achieves its high-performance runtime by compiling specialized versions of functions for particular types of arguments – a process that relies on type inference using data flow techniques. However, global variables can be written to at any time, and by any code. The compiler cannot keep track of all writes to the global variables; this would be akin to solving the halting problem. Therefore, the data-flow technique fails to perform any inference for these types of global variables. As a result, the compiler cannot create specialized functions when using these variables.

To understand the performance hit of using the global variables, let's use a simple function that calculates the sum of the integer powers of a set of floating point values:

1. First, we use a global variable to store the integer power:

```
p = 2

function pow_array(x::Vector{Float64})
    s = 0.0
    for y in x
        s = s + y^p
    end
    return s
end
```

2. Benchmarking this function, we see that it takes approximately 10 milliseconds for each evaluation of this function for an input array of length `100000`. This is way too high for something that should only take a few machine instructions to execute:

```
julia> t=rand(100000);

julia> @btime pow_array($t)
 8.648 ms (300000 allocations: 4.58 MiB)
33240.25981204582
```

We're trying to measure the effect of accessing a global variable in the `pow_array` function. But, you may have noticed that we call the function with the `t` parameter, which happens to be a global variable itself. To ensure that the access to that variable is not counted in the time measurement, we use the `$t` invocation. This ensures that the benchmarking macros call the function in a way that removes that overhead from the measurement.

3. A look at the `@code_warntype` output for this function shows us that the compiler has been unable to infer the type of result when working with the global variable, marking it as `Any`:

```
julia> @code_warntype pow_array(t)
Body::Any
1 ── %1 = (Base.arraylen)(x)::Int64
│     %2 = (Base.sle_int)(0, %1)::Bool
...
...
10 ── goto #6
11 ── %39 = φ (#9 => %20, #5 => 0.0)::Any
└───── return %39
```

This type then flows through the entire function, right up to the return value (as usual, any untyped variables, displayed in red in the REPL, are shown in bold).

Fixing performance issues with globals

A simple way to get the performance back is to declare the global variable a `const` declaration:

```
const p2 = 2
function pow_array2(x::Vector{Float64})
    s = 0.0
    for y in x
        s = s + y^p2
    end
    return s
end
```

This one change will get us a little under two orders of magnitude performance gain on the following function:

```julia
julia> @btime pow_array2($t)
  103.506 μs (0 allocations: 0 bytes)
33240.25981204582
```

Global const

The `const` declaration in Julia means something different from the similar keyword in C. In Julia, a global variable declared as `const` can change its value (a warning is printed). However, what it cannot do is change its type. Also, note that you cannot explicitly declare the type of a global variable. That is, an incantation, such as `x::Int64 = 2`, will raise an error when made in the global scope.

Once again, `@code_warntype` will show us that this function is now correctly type-inferred all the way through. Compare this output against the one from the function in the preceding section. You will notice that the return value of this function is being inferred as `Float64`:

```julia
julia> @code_warntype pow_array2(t)
Body::Float64
1 ── %1 = (Base.arraylen)(x)::Int64
...
...
10 ── goto #6
11 ── %39 = φ (#9 => %20, #5 => 0.0)::Float64
 └───      return %39
```

Another way to solve the issue of the global variable is to pass global as a function argument. A function argument can be type inferred; hence, the function specialization will be affected in the following case:

```julia
function pow_array3(x::Vector{Float64})
    return pow_array_inner(x, p)
end

function pow_array_inner(x, pow)
    s = 0.0
    for y in x
        s = s + y^pow
    end
    return s
end
```

Timing this code, we see that it is much faster than the original version:

```
julia> @btime pow_array3($t)
  2.605 ms (1 allocation: 16 bytes)
33342.35131922416
```

We have removed the global variable inside the loop, having converted it to a function parameter. Some overhead does remain from the access of the global variable at the top of the function. As a result, this is not as fast as the optimized version with the `const` global. However, this may well be a useful strategy in some situations.

Inlining

As we've mentioned before, idiomatic Julia code typically consists of many small functions. Unlike most other language implementations, some of the core primitives in the base library are also implemented in Julia. All of this means that the overhead of a function call needs to be as low as possible for performant Julia code. This is partly ensured due to some aggressive **inlining** performed by the Julia compiler.

Inlining is an optimization performed by a compiler, where the contents of a function or method are inserted directly into the body of the caller of that function. Thus, instead of making a function call, execution continues by directly implementing the operations of the called function/method within the caller's body.

In addition, quite a few compiler optimization techniques only operate within the body of a single function. Inlining allows the function body to be larger, and, therefore, allows these optimizations to be more effective within the program.

Compiler optimizations

Julia uses the LLVM compiler to generate machine code, which is finally run on the **Central Processing Unit (CPU)**. Most of the usual compiler optimization techniques that run on Julia code are performed by LLVM. The one major exception is inlining, which is performed by the Julia compiler itself before LLVM is invoked.

Default inlining

The Julia compiler automatically inlines functions that it considers inline-worthy. The compiler implements a set of heuristics to determine what to inline. Essentially, this boils down to small functions with deterministic types.

While inlining usually results in an increase in code speed, it also simultaneously increases the size of the generated code. Hence, a balance needs to be maintained. The heuristics are, therefore, tuned to maximize the performance of a typical Julia code without causing excessive bloating of the compiled code.

As an example, let's take a look at a simple set of functions, f and g:

```
function f(x)
    a=x*5
    b=a+3
end

g(x) = f(2*x)
```

We can then look at the processed **Abstract Syntax Tree (AST)** after the compiler has run its type inference and inlining passes using the @code_typed macro. The following output shows that the instructions of the f function is directly implemented in the body of the g function. There is no *invoke f* instruction in there. Instead, the %2 and %3 expressions implement the multiplication by 5 and the addition by 3, which are the two expressions in f:

```
julia> @code_typed g(3)
CodeInfo(
1 1 ─ %1 = (Base.mul_int)(2, x)::Int64   │ ¦  *
  │    %2 = (Base.mul_int)(%1, 5)::Int64  │ │ ¦  *
  │    %3 = (Base.add_int)(%2, 3)::Int64  │ │ ¦  +
  └───    return %3
) => Int64
```

The benefits of inlining can be seen more starkly if we inspect the LLVM **Intermediate Representation (IR)** generated for this function, which we can see by using the @code_llvm macro:

```
julia> @code_llvm g(3)

define i64 @julia_g_35455(i64) {
top:
  %1 = mul i64 %0, 10
  %2 = add i64 %1, 3
  ret i64 %2
}
```

We see that the first line of the function is `%1 = mul i64 %0, 10`. This line of the IR shows the argument of the function being multiplied by `10`. Look back at the source of the function—the argument is multiplied by `2` in the `g` function, and, subsequently, by `5` in the `f` function. The LLVM optimizer has recognized this and has consolidated these two operations into a single multiplication. This optimization has occurred by merging code across two different functions, and so couldn't have happened without inlining.

This illustrates one of the primary benefits of inlining. With inlining, function bodies become larger, and this provides many more opportunities for compiler optimization techniques to become applicable to the code within functions.

Controlling inlining

The Julia compiler has certain heuristics on which functions to inline and which should not be. These are typically based on the size of the function bodies in order to limit the increase in code size due to inlining. Sometimes, however, in performance-sensitive functions that are called many times in `inner` loops (for example, array indexers), we will want to override this heuristic if it fails. In other words, we will want to inline a function even when the compiler thinks it should not be inlined.

For this purpose, Julia provides the `@inline` macro. This macro needs to be placed in front of a function definition. When that function is called, its body will be placed inline at the location where it is called.

There is no call-site annotation to force inlining. We cannot inline a particular invocation of an otherwise normal function. The function itself can be marked with `@inline`, and not the callsite of the function. However, even then, the `@inline` macro is only a strong encouragement to the compiler to inline the function. The compiler always makes the final decision on whether to inline a function.

1. Let's demonstrate this with an example. We will modify the `f` function from the previous section, making it much more complex. We use the same `g` function as earlier:

```
function f(x)
    a=x*5
    b=a+3
    c=a-4
    if c < 0
        throw(DomainError())
    elseif c < 2
```

```
            d=c^3
        else
            d=c^2
        end
    end
```

2. This `f` function is now too long to be inlined by default, which we will verify by inspecting the `@code_typed` output of `g`. We can that the function definition of `g` contains a call to the `f` function:

```
julia> @code_typed g(3)
CodeInfo(
1 1 ─ %1 = (Base.mul_int)(2, x)::Int64
  │     %2 = invoke Main.f(%1::Int64)::Int64
  └───      return %2
) => Int64
```

3. We then define the same computation in a function that we declare with the `@inline` **macro:**

```
@inline function f_in(x)
    a=x*5
    b=a+3
    c=a-4
    if c < 0
        throw(DomainError())
    elseif c < 2
        d=c^3
    else
        d=c^2
    end
end

g_in(x) = f_in(2*x)
```

4. When we inspect the compiled AST for this function, it is apparent that the called function has been inlined into the caller:

```
julia> @code_typed g_in(3)
CodeInfo(
1 1 ─ %1 = (Base.mul_int)(2, x)::Int64
  │     %2 = (Base.mul_int)(%1, 5)::Int64
  │          (Base.add_int)(%2, 3)::Int64
  │     %4 = (Base.sub_int)(%2, 4)::Int64
  │     %5 = (Base.slt_int)(%4, 0)::Bool
  └───      goto #3 if not %5
  2 ─      (Main.DomainError)()::Union{}
```

```
       └── $(Expr(:unreachable))::Union{}
3 ── %9 = (Base.slt_int)(%4, 2)::Bool
  └── goto #5 if not %9
4 ── %11 = (Base.mul_int)(%4, %4)::Int64
  │    %12 = (Base.mul_int)(%11, %4)::Int64
  └── goto #6
5 ── %14 = (Base.mul_int)(%4, %4)::Int64
  └── goto #6 | |
6 ── %16 = φ (#4 => %12, #5 => %14)::Int64
  └── return %16
) => Int64
```

So, this code hopefully makes it apparent how powerful and important inlining is within the Julia compiler.

Disabling inlining

We've seen how useful inlining can be in optimizing our programs. However, in some situations, it may be useful to turn off all inlining. These can be during complex debugging sessions or while running a code coverage analysis. In any situation where you need to maintain direct correspondence between source lines of code and executing machine code, inlining can be problematic.

So, Julia provides an -inline=no command-line option to be used in these circumstances. Using this option will disable all inlining, including the ones marked with @inline. We should warn you that using this option makes all Julia code significantly slower, and it is rarely useful outside of developing and debugging the compiler itself. However, it is there if you need it in rare situations.

Globally disabling inlining is a very big hammer, to be used only in exceptional situations. However, sometimes we may want to force certain small functions to not be inlined, without changing the global settings. One reason to do so would be if we were using a function boundary to enforce type stability, as we saw in Chapter 3, *Types, Type Inference, and Stability*. In such cases, if the compiler decides to inline the function, our optimizations would be defeated.

In these situations, we would mark such a function with the `@noinline` macro to disable inlining:

1. As an example, let's start with the simple `f` function, which, as we showed earlier, is inlined by default. We will modify this to force the compiler to not inline it:

   ```
   @noinline function f_ni(x)
        a=x*5
        b=a+3
   end

   g_ni(x) = f_ni(2*x)
   ```

2. When defined with the `@noinline` annotation, this function is not inlined, even though it is well within the limits that are usually inlined:

   ```
   julia> @code_typed g_ni(3)
   CodeInfo(
   1 1 ─ %1 = (Base.mul_int)(2, x)::Int64
     │   %2 = invoke Main.f_ni(%1::Int64)::Int64
     └──      return %2
   ) => Int64
   ```

In summary, inlining is a very important technique used by the Julia compiler. In most cases, the default heuristics are very effective. However, in certain situations, controlling the inlining can provide large benefits for high-performance code.

Constant propagation

One very useful optimization that the Julia compiler implements when calling functions is called constant propagation. When a function is called with an argument that is known at compile time, the invocation can happen once at compile time, and the call is then replaced with a constant value at runtime. While we have seen some constant values being combined within a single function (with inlining), constant propagation occurs across a function call boundary – which means that this is a more complex, and powerful, optimization.

As a simple example to demonstrate constant propagation, we define a `sqr` function that takes one argument and then returns the square of that value. A second function, `sqr2`, calls the first function with a `2` literal as an argument:

```
sqr(x) = x * x

sqr2() = sqr(2)

julia> @code_typed sqr2()
CodeInfo(
1 ─ return 4
) => Int64
```

You'll see in the compiled output that when the `sqr2` function is called, it returns a constant value of `4`. The entire call to `sqr` has been replaced with a constant value. This replacement happens even though `sqr` is a function that takes an argument.

Constant propagation is likely to be applied only to functions that are pure – in other words, functions that do not have side effects. This means that these functions not only do not modify or mutate any of its arguments, but they also do not change any global state. For example, the `rand()` function does not take any argument, and so could, on first glance, be considered to be side-effect free. However, it does mutate the global random number generator state, and thus is not pure. In summary, writing small, pure functions provides the greatest opportunity for the compiler to optimize your code.

Using macros for performance

So far in this chapter, we have focused on making our functions run faster. But sometimes, the best way to make any code faster is to do less work. This involves either changing the algorithm or moving the computation to compile time, which leaves less work to do at runtime.

The Julia compilation process

For a dynamic language such as Julia, the terms compile time and runtime are not always clearly defined. In some sense, everything happens at runtime, because Julia code is usually not compiled ahead of time to a binary.

However, there are clearly divided processes that occur from when the code is read from disk to when it is finally executed on the CPU, which is shown in the following diagram:

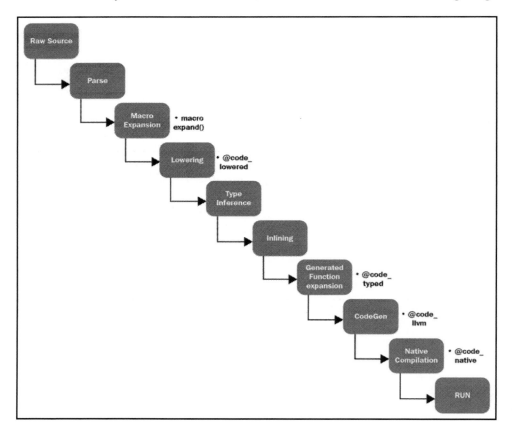

As the compiler goes through each stage, we can write code to execute at various points along this pipeline rather than everything waiting until the end, which is the traditional runtime. While we might loosely use the terminology of *compile time* for some of our meta-programming techniques, having the ability to run code at multiple stages along this pipeline provides some powerful capabilities.

Using macros

Julia macros are code that can be used to write other Julia code. A macro is executed very early in the compilation process, as soon as the code is loaded and parsed.

Macros are usually used as a means to reduce repetitive code, whereby large volumes of code with a common pattern can be generated from a smaller set of primitives. However, they can also be used to improve performance in some situations. This can be achieved by moving common or constant computation to the compile time wherever possible. To see how this can work, let's look at how we can evaluate a polynomial.

Evaluating a polynomial

Consider the following polynomial expression:

$$p(x) = \sum_{i=0}^{n} a_i x^i = a_0 + a_1 x + a_2 x^2 + a_3 x^3 + \cdots + a_n x^n$$

Given a set of coefficients $[a_0, a_1, a_2, ..., a_n]$, we need to find the value of the $p(x)$ function for a particular value of x:

1. A simple but general implementation to evaluate any polynomial may be as follows:

```
function poly_naive(x, a...)
   p=zero(x)
   for i = 1:length(a)
      p = p + a[i] *  x^(i-1)
   end
   return p
end
```

Type stability, once again
You will recognize this from the discussions in Chapter 3, *Types, Type Inference, and Stability*, that the initialization of p=zero(x) rather than p=0 ensures the type stability of this code.

2. Using this function, let's imagine that we need to compute a particular polynomial as follows:

$$f(x) = 1 + 2x + 3x^2 + 4x^3 + 5x^4 + 6x^5 + 7x^6 + 8x^7 + 9x^8$$

We do that in the f_naive function as follows:

```
f_naive(x) = poly_naive(x, 1,2,3,4,5,6,7,8,9)
```

3. Let's then benchmark the computation to see how fast it can run:

```
julia> x=3.5

julia> @btime f_naive($x)
  182.913 ns (0 allocations: 0 bytes)
271125.95703125
```

Note that we are splicing in the value of the input into the `f_naive` function when we benchmark it. If we call it directly as `@btime f_naive(3.5)`, constant propagation will optimize away the function call.

This computation takes a little over 180 nanoseconds. While this is not a particularly long interval, it is quite long for modern CPUs. A 2.4 GHz processor should be able to perform around 8,000 floating point operations in that time, which seems like a lot of work to compute a polynomial with five terms. The primary reason why this is slower than we would expect is that floating-point exponentiation is a particularly expensive operation.

Peak flops

The `peakflops()` Julia function will return the maximum number of **floating point operations per second (flops)** possible on the current processor.

Horner's method

So, the first thing to do is to find a better algorithm, one that can replace the exponentiation into multiplications. This can be done by Horner's method, which is named after the nineteenth-century British mathematician, William George Horner:

1. This is accomplished by defining a sequence, as follows:

$$b_n = a_n$$
$$b_{n-1} = a_{n-1} + b_n x$$
$$b_{n-2} = a_{n-2} + b_{n-1} x$$
$$\vdots$$
$$b_0 = a_0 + b_1 x$$

Here, b_0 is the value of the $p(x)$ polynomial.

2. This algorithm can be implemented in Julia, as follows:

```
function poly_horner(x, a...)
    b=zero(x)
    for i = length(a):-1:1
        b = a[i] + b * x
    end
    return b
end
```

3. We can then test and benchmark this for the same polynomial:

```
f_horner(x) = poly_horner(x, 1,2,3,4,5,6,7,8,9)

julia> @btime f_horner($x)
  6.438 ns (0 allocations: 0 bytes)
271125.95703125
```

We can see that using a better algorithm gets us a $30x$ improvement in the evaluation speed of this polynomial. Can we do better?

The Horner macro

Improving the speed of this computation starts with realizing that the coefficients of the polynomial are constants. They do not change and are known when writing the program. In other words, they are known at compile time. So, maybe we can expand and write out the expression for Horner's rule for our polynomial. This will take the following form for the polynomial that we used previously:

```
muladd(x,muladd(x,muladd(x,muladd(x,...,4),3),2),1)
```

This is likely to be the fastest way to compute our polynomial. However, writing this out for every polynomial that we might want to use will be extremely annoying. We lose the benefit of having a general library function that can compute any polynomial.

This is exactly the kind of situation where macros can help. We can write a macro that will produce the previous expression when given a set of polynomial coefficients. This can be done once when the compiler loads the code. At runtime, when this function is called, it will execute this optimized expression. Julia's base library contains this macro, which we can see repeated as follows:

```
macro horner(x, p...)
    ex = esc(p[end])
    for i = length(p)-1:-1:1
        ex = :(muladd(t, $ex, $(esc(p[i])))))
```

```
    end
    Expr(:block, :(t = $(esc(x))), ex)
end

f_horner_macro(x) = @horner(x, 1,2,3,4,5,6,7,8,9)

julia> @btime f_horner_macro($x)
  4.517 ns (0 allocations: 0 bytes)
271125.95703125
```

So, this method using a macro gives us a further improvement over calling the Horner's method as a function. This function also does not allocate any memory at runtime.

We've seen how this strategy of generating customized code for particular problems using a macro can sometimes lead to large performance increases. While the @horner macro is a simple and canonical example of this strategy, it can be used to great effect in our own code.

This example also shows that the speed of a language is not just about compiler techniques, or the quality of the code generated. While those are important, it is also important to provide the programmer primitives required for running a fast algorithm. However good the compiler is, a better algorithm will always beat it. Horner's method is one where a Julia implementation will often beat a C implementation, simply because Julia enables a better algorithm to be written easily.

Generated functions

Macros run very early in the compilers process when there is no information about how the program might execute. The inputs to a macro are, therefore, simply symbols and expressions – the textual tokens that make up a program. Given that a lot of Julia's powers come from its type system, it may be useful to have something like macros – code that generates code – at a point where the compiler has inferred the types of the variables and arguments in the program. Generated functions (also known as **staged functions**) fulfill this need.

Using generated functions

Declaring a generated function is simple. Instead of the usual function keyword, **generated functions** are declared with the appropriately named @generated function keyword. This declares a function that can be called normally from any point in the rest of the program.

Generated functions come in two parts, which are related to how they are executed. They are invoked once for each unique type of its arguments. At this point, the arguments themselves take the values of their types. The return value of this execution must be an expression that is used as the body of the function when called with values of these types. This cycle is executed each time the function is called with new types. The function is called with types as values once, and then the returned expression is used for all invocations with argument values of this type.

More on generated functions
In this section, we have quickly described how to write generated functions without going into too much detail. For more information along with examples, please refer to the online Julia documentation.

Using generated functions for performance

As with macros, strategies to use generated functions for performance revolve around moving constant parts of the computation earlier into the compilation stage. However, unlike macros, the computations depend on the type of arguments. For different types of argument, the different code can be executed. Staged functions handle this difference elegantly.

As an example, let's consider a rather contrived problem: calculating the number of cells of a multidimensional array. The answer is, of course, a product of the number of elements in each dimension. As Julia has true multidimensional arrays, the number of dimensions and the number of multiplications are not known upfront:

1. One possible implementation is to loop over the number of dimensions, multiplying as we go:

```
function prod_dim(x::Array{T, N}) where {T, N}
    s = 1
    for i = 1:N
        s = s * size(x, i)
    end
    return s
end
```

Type parameters
Please review the official Julia documentation on type parameters or refer to the *Type parameters* section in `Chapter 3`, *Types, Type Inference, and Stability*, if the preceding code looks unfamiliar.

2. This function will now work for arrays with any number of dimensions. Let's test this to see whether it works:

```julia
julia> prod_dim(rand(10, 5, 5))
250
```

3. Optimizing this computation with a generated function starts with the observation that the number of iterations of the loop is equal to the number of dimensions of the array, which is encoded as a `type` parameter for arrays. In other words, for a particular type of input (an array of a particular dimension), the loop size is fixed. So, what we can try to do in a generated function is move the loop to the compile time:

```julia
@generated function prod_dim_gen{T, N}(x::Array{T, N})
    ex = :(1)
    for i in 1:N
        ex = :(size(x, $i) * $ex)
    end
    return ex
end
```

4. In this generated function, the loop runs at compile time when the type of `x` is known. We create an `ex` expression, which then becomes the body of the function when actually called with an instance of an array. We can see that this function works; it returns the same result as our earlier version with the loop:

```julia
julia> prod_dim_gen(rand(10, 5, 5))
250
```

5. It would, however, be instructive to see the code that is generated and actually run it for this function. For this purpose, we can paste the body of the generated function into a normal function, as follows:

```julia
function prod_dim_gen_impl(x::Array{T, N}) where {T,N}
    ex = :(1)
    for i in 1:N
        ex = :(size(x, $i) * $ex)
    end
    return ex
end
```

6. We can then call this function with the type of the arguments as input, and the returned expression will show us how this generated function works:

```julia
julia> x = rand(10, 5, 5);

julia> prod_dim_gen_impl(x)
:(size(x, 3) * (size(x, 2) * (size(x, 1) * 1)))

julia> x = rand(10, 5, 5, 2);

julia> prod_dim_gen_impl(x)
:(size(x, 4) * (size(x, 3) * (size(x, 2) * (size(x, 1) * 1))))
```

It should be apparent what has happened here. For an array of three dimensions, we are multiplying three numbers, while, for an array of four dimensions, we are multiplying two numbers. The loop of 1:N ran at compile time and then disappeared. The resulting code will be much faster without the loop, particularly if this function is called excessively in some other inner loop.

The technique of removing loops and replacing them with the calculations inline is usually called **loop-unrolling**, and it is often performed manually in performance-sensitive code. However, in Julia, generated functions are an easy and elegant way to achieve this without too much effort.

You should also note that this function looks much simpler without the loop. The number of tokens in this function is significantly reduced. This might make the function inline-worthy and cause the compiler to inline this function, making this code even faster.

Using keyword arguments

Julia supports a convenient keyword argument syntax that is useful when creating a complicated API with many optional parameters. However, there is a slight overhead associated with keyword arguments, which means that their use should be minimized in performance-sensitive inner loops.

As an example, we will write the same function twice, once with keyword arguments, and once with regular, positional arguments. It will be apparent that the version with keyword arguments does not perform as well:

```
named_param(x; y=1, z=1) = x^y + x^z

pos_param(x,y,z) = x^y + x^z

julia> @btime named_param(4; y=2, z=3)
  8.306 ns (0 allocations: 0 bytes)
80

julia> @btime pos_param(4, 2, 3)
  5.548 ns (0 allocations: 0 bytes)
80
```

We see that using named parameters a incurs significant overhead in Julia. However, when designing high-level functions, it is still advantageous to use named parameters in order to create easy to use APIs. Just don't use them in performance-sensitive `inner` loops.

Summary

In this chapter, we looked at different ways to structure our code to make it perform better. The function is the primary element in Julia code; however, sometimes it is not the best option. Macros and generated functions can play an important role where appropriate.

In the next chapter, we will look deeper into the problem of numbers. We will see how Julia designs its core number types, and how to make basic numeric operations fly.

5
Fast Numbers

As a numerical programming language, fast computations with numbers are central to everything we do in Julia. In the previous chapters, we discussed how the Julia compiler and runtime perform across a wide range of code. In this chapter, we will take a focused look at how the core numerical constructs are designed and implemented in Julia.

In this chapter, we will cover the following topics:

- Numbers in Julia, their layout, and storage
- Trading performance for accuracy
- Subnormal numbers

Numbers in Julia, their layout, and storage

The basic number types in Julia are designed to closely follow the hardware on which it runs. Integers and floats, therefore, have the same behavior as that which is defined in the CPU hardware, and operations on them run at hardware speeds. The decision to have default numeric types that are as close to the metal as possible is something that contributes to the C-like speed of Julia.

Integers

Integers in Julia are stored as system integers, which means that they are values that the CPU considers to be integers. The internal representation is what you would expect in C. Their default size, as in C, depends on the size of the CPU/OS on which Julia runs. On a 32-bit OS, the integers are 32 bits by default, and on a 64-bit machine, they are 64 bits by default.

These two integer sizes are represented as different types within Julia: `Int32` and `Int64`, respectively. The `Int` type alias represents the actual integer type used by the system. On a 32-bit system, `Int` refers to `Int32`, while on a 64-bit system, `Int` refers to `Int64`. The `WORD_SIZE` constant can also be queried to determine the bit width of the current Julia environment:

```
julia> Sys.WORD_SIZE
64
```

The `bitstring` function displays the underlying binary representation of the numbers. On a 64-bit machine, we get the following:

```
julia> bitstring(3)
"0000000000000000000000000000000000000000000000000000000000000011"
```

The default integer types are signed; that is, the first (or the most significant) bit is set to one to denote negative numbers, which are then stored as two's complement, as follows:

```
julia> bitstring(-3)
"1111111111111111111111111111111111111111111111111111111111111101"
```

To get a two's complement representation of a number, you invert all digits (that is, 0 becomes 1, and 1 becomes 0) and add 1 to the result.

Types such as integers and floats, whose representations are simply a set of bits, have optimized handling within the Julia runtime. They are called **bits types**, and this feature can be queried for any type using the `isbitstype` function, as follows:

```
julia> isbitstype(Int64)
true

julia> isbitstype(String)
false
```

One point to note is that when stored as a Julia value, basic numeric types can be boxed. This means that when numeric types are stored in the memory of the computer, they are prefixed with a tag that represents their type. However, the Julia compiler is usually very good at removing any unnecessary boxing/unboxing operations. They can usually be compiled out in the native code that goes to the CPU. For example, we can define a function that adds two numbers, and inspect the machine code that is generated and executed when this function is called through the following code:

```
myadd(x, y) = x + y
```

Boxing:
This is the process of converting a raw numeric value into a typed object. Take a set of bits in the memory of the computer. Boxing is the process of adding extra information so that Julia knows it is an object of type `Int64`.

Unboxing:
This is the reverse process—removing extra information about a type to extract the raw value.

When looking at the output of the following compiled code, even if, like me, you are not an expert at reading assembly, it should be apparent that other than the function overhead to set the stack and return the result, the generated code simply consists of the **Load Effective Address Quad** (`leaq`) CPU instruction, which essentially adds two 4-byte numbers. Depending on your CPU and Julia/LLVM version, you may see other instructions here, such as `addq`, but the important thing to note is that there is no boxing/unboxing operation remaining in the native code when the function is called:

```
julia> @code_native myadd(1,2)
    leaq (%rdi,%rsi), %rax
    retq
    nopw %cs:(%rax,%rax)
```

There is an even bigger advantage to storing numbers using the machine representation. Arrays of these numbers can be stored using contiguous storage. A type tag is stored once at the start. Beyond this, data in numerical arrays is stored in a packed form. This is the representation of arrays that is expected by C-language programs. Therefore, not only can these arrays can be passed to C libraries directly (without copying), but the compiler can also optimize computations on these arrays easily—the inner loop can operate directly on the raw, unboxed types. There is no need for pointer dereferencing when operating on numerical arrays of bit types.

Integer overflow

Not only does Julia use machine representation to store integers and floats, it also uses machine arithmetic for all basic mathematical operations. In particular, the operations on integer types do not perform overflow checks. Let's discuss what this means in practice.

With a fixed number of bytes available to represent integers of a particular type, the possible values are bounded. These bounds can be viewed using the `typemax` and `typemin` functions:

```
julia> typemax(Int64)
9223372036854775807

julia> bitstring(typemax(Int32))
"01111111111111111111111111111111111111111111111111111111111111111"

julia> typemin(Int64)
-9223372036854775808

julia> bitstring(typemin(Int32))
"10000000000000000000000000000000000000000000000000000000000000000"
```

When the result of any operation is beyond the possible values for a type, it overflows. This typically results in the number being wrapped around from the maximum to the minimum, as in the following code (refer back to the maximum and minimum values of `Int64` while reading the following expressions):

```
julia> 9223372036854775806 + 1
9223372036854775807

julia> 9223372036854775806 + 1 + 1
-9223372036854775808
```

This code demonstrates that when we add one to the maximum possible value of an `Int64` instance, we get a value equal to the minimum possible value for `Int64` instances.

Another way to think about an overflow is that to represent larger numbers, additional bits are required in the most significant positions. These bits are then chopped off, and the remaining bits are returned as a result. Thinking about it in this way explains many counter-intuitive results when it comes to overflows. Take a look at the following code:

```
julia> 2^62
4611686018427387904

julia> 2^63
-9223372036854775808

julia> 2^64
0

julia> 2^65
0
```

This behavior is different from what is observed in popular dynamic languages, such as Ruby and Python. In these languages, every basic mathematical operation includes an overflow check. When the overflow is detected, the value is automatically upgraded to a wider type that is capable of storing the larger value. However, this causes a significant overhead to all numerical computation. Not only do we have to pay the cost of the extra CPU operation for the overflow check, but the conditional statement also prevents CPU pipelining from being effective. For this reason, Julia (as with Java and C) chooses to operate directly on machine integers and forgo all overflow checks.

At first glance, this may seem confusing and frustrating if you have a background in programming Python or Ruby, but this is the price you pay for high-performance computing.

I must say that in practice, this is rarely a problem in the majority of the applications that I have experienced. You'll almost never have use cases where the full precision of Int64 is required, while still having the possibility of unbounded numbers. Integers are used for countable things, and very few applications need to count things beyond 9 quintillion. For domains where larger numbers are possible, this is usually known upfront. One example of such a domain might be pure number theory. In those situations, the design usually calls for a different representation, such as BigInt, or even a custom type.

BigInt (which is covered in the following section) can seem like a solution to this problem—so why not use the BigInt type all the time? Well, because they are orders of magnitude slower than regular integers, and thus are not practicable in most situations. However, as we said previously, in some use cases, they are perfect.

If you want to be in a situation where you must absolutely guarantee that numbers do not overflow, but cannot pay the performance cost of BigInt, consider using floats. Floats can contain arbitrarily large numbers, simply by reducing the precision at which they store the values. And while the possible lack of precision in floating point numbers may seem unacceptable at first, note that a floating point number stores exact representations of integers up to 52 bits in size. In other words, up to 52 bits (about 4 quadrillion), integers and floats have the same precision.

Yet another option to consider when you cannot have overflows and underflows in your code is the SaferInteger package. When you use the number types from this package, any overflow and underflow will throw an error. In other words, all numeric operations are checked for overflow and underflow. Once again, this has a significant performance cost, and hence, we will not spend any more time on it in this book. However, it can be very useful if you need it. More details are available on the project page, at https://github.com/JeffreySarnoff/SaferIntegers.jl.

Once you understand that Julia's numbers are really close to the metal, and are designed to be directly operated on by the CPU, it is not very difficult to construct correctly behaving programs in practice.

BigInt

As we saw in the previous section, if you know your program needs to operate on large integers beyond the range of Int32 or Int64, there are various options in Julia. First, if your numbers can still be bounded, there is Int128. However, for arbitrarily large integers, Julia has built-in support via the BigInt type. Run the following code to see the difference from the normal bounded integers (and compare the results to the previous section where we added the large integers.):

```
julia> big(9223372036854775806) + 1 + 1
9223372036854775808

julia> big(2)^64
18446744073709551616
```

Operations on Int128 are similar in performance, while for BigInt types they are much slower than for the basic integers. In the following code, we measure the time for the creation and multiplication of two integers in different forms:

```
julia> x = rand(Int32)
-1509689045

julia> y = rand(Int32)
-1296681900

julia> @btime $(BigInt(y)) * $(BigInt(x)) ;
  151.894 ns (3 allocations: 48 bytes)

julia> @btime $(Int64(y)) * $(Int64(x)) ;
  0.030 ns (0 allocations: 0 bytes)

julia> @btime $(Int128(y)) * $(Int128(x)) ;
  0.030 ns (0 allocations: 0 bytes)

julia> @btime $(Int32(y)) * $(Int32(x)) ;
  0.030 ns (0 allocations: 0 bytes)
```

Operations on `Int128` are slower, and for `BigInts` they are much slower than for the basic integers. However, we can use them in situations where they are warranted, without compromising on the performance of computations that fit within the bounds of the default types.

The floating point

The default floating point type is always 64 bits wide and is called `Float64`. This is true irrespective of the underlying machine and OS bit width. It is represented in the computer's memory using the **Institute of Electrical and Electronics Engineers (IEEE)** 754 binary standard. Once again, this storage format is the same as the numbers in C; these are low-level machine types.

The IEEE 754 standard is the universally accepted technical standard for floating point operations in computer hardware and software. Almost all commonly used CPU types implement their floating point support in their hardware using this standard. As a result, storing numbers in this format means that the CPU (or rather the **FPU—the floating point unit** within the CPU) can operate on them natively and quickly.

The binary storage standard for the 64-bit floating point numbers consists of 1 sign bit, 11 bits of exponent, and 52 bits of the mantissa (or the significand). The internal storage can be seen using the `bitstring` function:

```
julia> bitstring(2.5)
"0100000000000100000000000000000000000000000000000000000000000000"

julia> bitstring(-2.5)
"1100000000000100000000000000000000000000000000000000000000000000"
```

The layout of the bits can be better visualized if we define a simple function to print the values as they are stored. This makes clear the three parts that make up a floating point number:

```
function floatbits(x::Float64)
    b = bitstring(x)
    b[1:1]*"|"*b[2:12]*"|"*b[13:end]
end

julia> floatbits(2.5)
"0|10000000000|0100000000000000000000000000000000000000000000000000"

julia> floatbits(-2.5)
"1|10000000000|0100000000000000000000000000000000000000000000000000"
```

The first bit is interpreted such that the number is positive if it is zero, and negative if it is one. The next 11 bits (looking from left to right as written, or from the most significant to the least) are the exponent. This is interpreted as 2^{n-1023}. In this case, this is 10000000000 in binary, and 1,024 in decimal. Thus, the value of the exponent is $2^{1024-1023}$ which is 2^1, or *2*.

The next 53 bits are known as the significand (or sometimes the mantissa, although this term is no longer recommended, since it has multiple meanings). This set of bits is interpreted as a binary fraction: $1.b_1b_2b_3 \ldots b_{52}$. In other words, this represents the real number: $1 + b_1/2 + b_2/4 + b_{3/8} + \ldots + b_{52}/2^{52}$. Thus, for our number above, the value of the significand is *1+ 0/2 + 1/4*, which is *1.25*. Putting all three parts of the number together, we get *1 * 2 * 1.25*, which gives us the original number, *2.5*.

Floating point accuracy

All the issues around accuracy, precision, and rounding errors are the result of one fundamental feature—not all decimal numbers are exactly representable as binary floating point numbers, and many decimal values can be approximated by the same float.

For example, consider the floating point number, 0.1. In traditional mathematics, this is equal to the rational number of one-tenth, or in other words, equal to 1 divided by 10. However, as demonstrated in the following code, the decimal number, 0.1, cannot be exactly represented in binary form in 64 bits using the formulation we saw in the previous section:

```
julia> 0.1 > 1//10
true

julia> Rational(0.1)
3602879701896397//36028797018963968
```

When we convert the floating point value to its fractional form, we see that it is very different from one-tenth (though very near in magnitude). When we try to get an accurate decimal representation of this number, it turns out to be slightly larger than 0.1:

```
julia> float(big(Rational(0.1)))
1.000000000000000055511151231257827021181583404541015625e-01
```

Looking at this another way, we can see that the underlying storage of two very close numbers are the same, which means they cannot be distinguished in the code:

```
julia> bitstring(0.10000000000000001) == bitstring(0.1)
true
```

And that brings us to the concept of machine epsilon or **eps**. This refers to the difference between two floating numbers, where any number between those two cannot be represented as a binary floating point number:

```
julia> eps(0.1)
1.3877787807814457e-17
```

This means that a number between 0.1 and ($0.1 + 1.3877 \times 10^{-17}$) cannot be represented as `Float64`. In other words, making the smallest change to the binary representation of 0.1 will give the second number—nothing in between can be stored. This second number, the next largest float that one can get, can be retrieved by the `nextfloat` function:

```
julia> nextfloat(0.1)
0.10000000000000002
```

We see that the next float after 0.1 is 0.10000000000000002; this is more than 0.1000000000000001, which as we saw previously, is indistinguishable from 0.1. The difference between two nearby floats should be the smallest possible change. This means adding 1 to the least significant digit, the **unit in last place** (**ULP**). Comparing the bits in these numbers, we see that this is true:

```
julia> floatbits(0.1)
"0|01111111011|1001100110011001100110011001100110011001100110011010"

julia> floatbits(nextfloat(0.1))
"0|01111111011|1001100110011001100110011001100110011001100110011011"
```

The ULP is thus the difference between the two nearest floating point numbers. It is a measure of the space of numbers that cannot be represented exactly on the computer. It is how the accuracy of mathematical operations on floating point numbers are benchmarked.

Unsigned integers

The basic integers described previously are all signed values, in that numbers greater and less than zero are stored separately. Unsigned integers can be stored using the `UInt64` and `UInt32` types. As with many other Julia types, the type conversions can be done via constructors, as follows:

```
julia> UInt64(1)
0x0000000000000001
```

Unsigned integers can be created as literals when written in hexadecimal or binary form; for example, 0x9E or 0b10011001, respectively.

These conversions check for out-of-range values. They throw an error when trying to convert a value that does not fit in the resulting type, as follows:

```
julia> UInt32(4294967297)
ERROR: InexactError: trunc(UInt32, 4294967297)
Stacktrace:
....
```

The conditional check will have an overhead when performing this calculation, not only as a result of carrying out the CPU's instructions, but also because of pipeline failures due to branching. In some situations, when working with binary data, it may be acceptable to truncate 64-bit values to 32-bit values without checking. In such situations, there is a shortcut in Julia, which is to use the % operator with the type, as in the following code:

```
julia> 4294967297 % UInt32
0x00000001
```

Using this construct prevents any errors from being thrown for out-of-bounds values, and it is much faster than the checked version of the conversion. Benchmarking the two conversions, we see that the unchecked conversion is about twice as fast as the checked version:

```
julia> @btime UInt32(1)
  0.065 ns (0 allocations: 0 bytes)
0x00000001

julia> @btime 1 % UInt32
  0.032 ns (0 allocations: 0 bytes)
0x00000001
```

This also works for other base unsigned types, such as UInt16 and UInt8.

Trading performance for accuracy

In this book, we largely focus on performance; that is, how to make your computations faster. However, it probably goes without saying that it does not matter how fast a function returns, if it returns the wrong result. At some point, accuracy has to override performance.

The Julia compiler and standard library has been written with particular attention to the accuracy of numerical operations. All basic floating point arithmetic in Julia follows strict IEEE 754 semantics. Rounding is handled carefully in all base library code to guarantee the theoretical best error limits. Basic mathematical operations and functions are guaranteed to be accurate to within 1 ULP.

However, algorithms do not always require the full precision of the IEEE rules, and demand higher performance. In these situations, it is possible to trade some accuracy for performance.

The @fastmath macro

The @fastmath macro is a tool that can be used to loosen the constraints of IEEE floating point operations in order to achieve greater performance. The macro replaces a fixed set of about 50 mathematical operations with faster implementations. In doing so, it can rearrange the order of evaluation to something which is mathematically equivalent, but that would not be the same for discrete floating point numbers due to rounding effects. It can also replace some intrinsic operations with their faster variants that do not check for NaN or Infinity. This results in faster execution, but with a corresponding reduction in accuracy. This option is similar to the -ffast-math option in the Clang or GCC compilers.

For example, consider the following code that calculates the finite difference between the elements of an array and then sums them. We can create two versions of the function that are identical, except for the fact that one has the @fastmath annotation and one doesn't. First, the normal version for the function:

```
function sum_diff(x)
    n = length(x)
    d = 1/(n-1)
    s = zero(eltype(x))
    s = s +  (x[2] - x[1]) / d
    for i in 2:length(x)-1
        s =  s + (x[i+1] - x[i+1]) / (2*d)
    end
    s = s + (x[n] - x[n-1])/d
end
```

Next, the same function, but with @fastmath annotations:

```
function sum_diff_fast(x)
    n=length(x)
    d = 1/(n-1)
    s = zero(eltype(x))
```

```
    @fastmath s = s + (x[2] - x[1]) / d
    @fastmath for i in 2:n-1
                s = s + (x[i+1] - x[i+1]) / (2*d)
            end
    @fastmath s = s + (x[n] - x[n-1])/d
end
```

We can note that the @fastmath macro can be used in front of statements or loops. In fact, it can be used in front of any block of code, including functions. Anything that is relevant within this block will be rewritten by the macro to use faster implementations.

Benchmarking the two implementations shows an improvement in performance greater than tenfold from the base version with @fastmath, while losing only a digit of precision:

```
julia> t=rand(2000);

julia> @btime sum_diff($t)
  6.813 μs (0 allocations: 0 bytes)
453.97858245810266


julia> @btime sum_diff_fast($t)
  704.803 ns (0 allocations: 0 bytes)
453.9785824581026
```

This result is very much dependent on the nature of the computation. In many situations, the improvements are much lower. Also, in this case, loss of precision is relatively low, which may not be true in every case. The advice, then, is to test and measure extensively when using this feature.

As with everything else in Julia, we can inspect the changes that the macro makes to our code. We can observe that the macro rewrites the intrinsic functions with its own _fast versions:

```
julia> macroexpand(Main, :(@fastmath a + b / c))
:((Base.FastMath).add_fast(a, (Base.FastMath).div_fast(b, c)))
```

Sometimes the use of the @fastmath macro can not only lead to faster code, but also a more elegant design. Consider a function that halves its input, and another that doubles it. A function that composes these two functions (calls them one after the other) will just return the original input, since the multiplications by 2 and then again by 0.5 should cancel each other out.

However, note that floating point multiplication itself is not associative, even though multiplication on the real number line is associative. In other words, `(a*b)*c` is not the same as `a*(b*c)`, since the rounding errors can be different in either case. The rounding errors depend on the relative sizes of a, b, and c, and hence, the compiler cannot cancel out the successive multiplications by 0.5 and 2. However, using the `@fastmath` macro allows the multiplication to be re-ordered, and thus optimized:

```
half_fast(x) = @fastmath 0.5*x

double_fast(x) = @fastmath 2.0*x

julia> const c_fast = (half_fast ∘ double_fast)
#52 (generic function with 1 method)

julia> @code_llvm c_fast(0.0)
define double @"julia_#52_35697"(double) {
top:
  ret double %0
}
```

The (∘) operator composes two functions, creating a new function that applies each of its components successively. It can by typed using `\circ<TAB>`.

Looking at the compiled code, we see that the function has been optimized to return its input directly, with both multiplications having been optimized out. Comparing this with a comparable set of functions without the `@fastmath` annotations makes this apparent:

```
@code_llvm

half(x) = 0.5*x
double(x) = 2*x
c(x) = half(double(x))

julia> @code_llvm c(0.0)
define double @"julia_#52_35637"(double) {
top:
  %1 = fmul double %0, 2.000000e+00
  %2 = fmul double %1, 5.000000e-01
  ret double %2
}
```

These functions might feel contrived, but consider that a multiplication by two can arise out of differentiating the x^2 function. A multiplication by 0.5 might arise out of a scaling function. Both of these could be defined and applied separately, in a completely general way. However, in special cases, the compiler can optimize the computation significantly without any effort on the developer, or any loss of generality. In Julia, abstractions often have no runtime cost—this is one of the most powerful effects of its design.

The K-B-N summation

Adding a collection of floating point values is a very common operation, but it is surprisingly susceptible to the accumulation of errors. A naïve implementation—adding the list from the first element to the last—accumulates errors at the rate of $O(\sqrt{n})$, where n is the number of elements being summed. Julia's sum base uses a pairwise summation algorithm that does better by accumulating errors at $O\left(\sqrt{\log(n)}\right)$, but is almost as fast. However, there exists a more complicated summation algorithm attributed to William Kahan—the K-B-N summation—whose error is bound by $O(1)$. This is implemented in Julia by the sum_kbn function. In order to test the accuracy of sum, we will use a set of numbers that are particularly susceptible to rounding errors. The sum of the set of three numbers (1, -1, and 10^{-100}) should be 10^{-100}. However, as one of these numbers is much smaller than the other two, the result will be incorrectly rounded to zero:

```julia
julia> t=[1, -1, 1e-100];

julia> sum(t)
0.0

julia> using Pkg; Pkg.add("KahanSummation")

julia> using KahanSummation

julia> sum_kbn(t)
1.0e-100
```

So we see that Kahan summation is is more accurate. However, it is also much slower:

```julia
julia> @btime sum($t)
  4.207 ns (0 allocations: 0 bytes)
1.0e-100

julia> @btime sum_kbn($t)
  11.311 ns (0 allocations: 0 bytes)
1.0e-100
```

In summary, the default `sum` function is adequate for most situations. It is fast and quite accurate. However, for pathological cases or when summing millions of elements, the `sum_kbn` function may give up some performance for increased accuracy.

Subnormal numbers

Subnormal numbers (also sometimes called **denormal numbers**) are very small floating point values, near zero. Formally, they are numbers *smaller* than those that can be represented without leading zeros in the significand.

Typically, floating point numbers are represented without leading zeros in the significand. Leading zeros in the number are moved to the exponent (that is, *0.0123* is represented as *1.23×10^{-2}*). Subnormal numbers are, however numbers in which such a representation would cause the exponent to be lower than the minimum possible value. In such a situation, the significand is forced to have leading zeros.

Subnormal numbers in Julia can be identified by the `issubnormal` function, as follows:

```
julia> issubnormal(1.0)
false

julia> issubnormal(1.0e-308)
true
```

Subnormal numbers are useful for a gradual underflow. Without them, for example, subtraction between extremely small values of floating point numbers might underflow to zero, causing subsequent *divide-by-zero* errors. This is shown in the following code:

```
julia> 3e-308 - 3.001e-308
-1.0e-311

julia> issubnormal(3e-308 - 3.001e-308)
true
```

Subnormal numbers to zero

Subnormal numbers cause a significant slowdown on modern CPUs. Worse, this may be hard to track down because these performance problems can occur only when the inputs take certain values. For the same algorithm, the problem may manifest as unexplained, intermittent slowdowns. Computations are fast for some inputs, but slow for other values of inputs.

One solution would be to force all subnormal numbers to be treated as zero. This will set a CPU flag that discards all the subnormal numbers and uses zeros in its place. While this solves the performance problem, it should be used with care, as it may cause accuracy and numerical stability problems. In particular, it is no longer true that $x-y = 0 => x = y$, as we can see in the following code:

```
julia> set_zero_subnormals(true)
true

julia> 3e-308 - 3.001e-308
-0.0

julia> 3e-308 == 3.001e-308
false

julia> get_zero_subnormals()
true
```

One of the ways subnormal numbers arise is when a calculation exponentially decays to zero. This gradual flattening of the curve results in many subnormal numbers being created and causes a sudden performance drop. As an example, we will take a look at an algorithm to compute the heat-flow over a conductor. First, define a function that computes a single time step:

```
function timestep( b, a, dt )
    n = length(b)
    b[1] = 1
    two = eltype(b)(2)
    for i=2:n-1
        b[i] = a[i] + (a[i-1] - two*a[i] + a[i+1]) * dt
    end
    b[n] = 0
end
```

Then define a function that computes heatflow over a certain number of steps:

```
function heatflow( a, nstep )
    b = similar(a)
    o = eltype(a)(0.1)
    for t=1:div(nstep,2)
        timestep(b,a,o)
        timestep(a,b,o)
    end
end
```

We can then benchmark these functions with and without forcing subnormal numbers to zero. Take a look at the following:

```
julia> set_zero_subnormals(false)
true

julia> t=rand(1000);

julia> @btime heatflow($t, 1000)
  1.559 ms (1 allocation: 7.94 KiB)

julia> set_zero_subnormals(true)
true

julia> @btime heatflow($t, 1000)
  1.062 ms (1 allocation: 7.94 KiB)
```

We can see a significant increase in speed by forcing subnormal numbers to zero.

Summary

In this chapter, we discussed how Julia uses a machine representation of numbers to achieve a C-like performance for its arithmetic computations. We noted how to work within these design constraints, and considered the edge cases that are introduced.

Working with single numbers, however, is the easy part. Most numerical computations, as we noted throughout this chapter, consist of working on large sets of numbers. In the next chapter, we will take a look at how to work with arrays in a performant manner.

6
Using Arrays

It should not be a surprise to the reader of this book that array operations are often the cornerstone of scientific and numeric programming. While arrays are a fundamental data structure in all programming, there are special considerations to bear in mind when used in numerical programming. One particular difference is that arrays are not just viewed as entities for data storage. Rather, they may represent the fundamental mathematical structures of vectors and matrices.

In this chapter, we will discuss how to use arrays in Julia in the fastest possible way. When you profile your program, you will find that in many cases, the majority of its execution time is spent in array operations. Therefore, the discussions in this chapter will likely turn out to be crucial in creating high-performance Julia code. The following are the topics we will cover:

- Array internals and storage
- Bounds checks
- In-place operations
- Broadcasting
- Subarrays and array views
- SIMD parallelization using AVX
- Specialized array types
- Writing generic library functions using arrays

Array internals in Julia

We discussed how Julia's performance comes out of using *type* information to compile specific and fast machine code for different data types. Nowhere is this more apparent than in array-related code. This is probably the use case in which all of Julia's design choices pay off for creating high-performance code.

Array representation and storage

The array type in Julia is parameterized by the type of its elements and the number of its dimensions. Hence, the type of an array is represented as `Array{T, N}`, where `T` is the type of its elements, and `N` is the number of dimensions. So, for example, `Array{UTF8String, 1}` is a one-dimensional array of strings, while `Array{Float64,2}` is a two-dimensional array of floating point numbers.

Type parameters

You must have realized that type parameters in Julia do not always have to be other types; they can be symbols, or instances of any bitstype. This makes Julia's type system enormously powerful. It allows the type system to represent complex relationships and enables many operations to be moved to compile (or dispatch) time, rather than at runtime.

Representing the type of its element within the type of arrays as a type parameter allows powerful optimization. It allows arrays of primitive types (and many immutable types) to be stored inline. In other words, the elements of the array are stored within the array's own primary memory allocation.

In the following diagram, we illustrate this storage mechanism. The numbers in the top row represent array indexes, while the numbers in the boxes are the integer elements stored within the array. The number in the bottom row represent the memory addresses where each of these elements are stored:

Index	1	2	3	4	5	6
Value	34	55	63	23	45	11
Address	1000	1004	1008	1012	1016	1020

In most other dynamic languages, all the arrays are stored using pointers to their values. This is usually because the language runtime does not have enough information about the types of values to be stored in an array, and hence, cannot allocate the correctly sized storage.

As represented in the following diagram, when an array is allocated, the contiguous storage simply consists of pointers to the actual elements, even when these elements are primitive types that can be stored natively in memory:

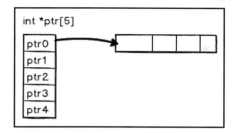

This method of storing arrays inline without pointer indirection as much as possible has many advantages and, as we discussed earlier, is responsible for many of Julia's performance claims. In other dynamic languages, the type of every element of the array is uncertain and the compiler has to insert type checks on each access. This can quickly add up and become a major performance drain.

Further, even when every element of the array is of the same type, we pay the cost of memory load for every array element if they are stored as pointers. Given the relative costs of a CPU operation versus a memory load on a modern processor, not doing this is a huge benefit.

There are other benefits too. When the compiler and CPU notice operations on a contiguous block of memory, CPU pipelining and caching are much more efficient. Some CPU optimizations, such as **Single Instruction Multiple Data (SIMD)**, are also unavailable when using indirect array loads.

Column-wise storage

When an array has only one dimension, its elements can be stored one after the other in a contiguous block of memory. As we observed in the previous section, operating on this array sequentially from its starting index to its end can be very fast, making it amenable to many compiler and CPU optimizations.

Two-dimensional (or greater) arrays can, however, be stored in two different ways. We can store them row-wise or column wise. In other words, we can store from the beginning of the array the elements of the first row, followed by the elements of the second row, and so on. Alternatively, we can store the elements of the first column, then the elements of the second column, and so on.

Consider, in the following diagram, the matrix with three rows and four columns:

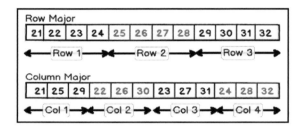

This matrix can be stored in two different ways, as illustrated in the following diagram. In the **Row Major** option, the elements of a row are stored together. In the **Column Major** option, the elements of a column are stored together:

Arrays in C are stored as row-ordered. Julia, on the other hand, chooses the latter strategy, storing arrays as column-ordered, similar to MATLAB and Fortran. This rule generalizes to the higher-dimensional array as well; it is always the last dimension that is stored first.

Naming conventions

Conventionally, the term *row* refers to the first dimension of a two-dimensional array, and *column* refers to the second dimension. As an example, for a two-dimensional array of x::Array{Float64, 2} floats, the expression x[2,4] refers to the elements in the second row and fourth column.

This particular strategy of storing arrays has implications for how we navigate them. The most efficient way to read an array is in the same order in which it is laid out in memory. That is, each sequential read should access contiguous areas in memory.

We can demonstrate the performance impact of reading arrays in sequence with the following code that squares and sums the elements of a two-dimensional floating point array, writing the result at each step back to the same position. The following code exercises both the read and write operations for the array:

```
function col_iter(x)
    s=zero(eltype(x))
    for i in 1:size(x, 2)
        for j in 1:size(x, 1)
            s = s + x[j, i] ^ 2
            x[j, i] = s
        end
    end
end

function row_iter(x)
    s=zero(eltype(x))
    for i in 1:size(x, 1)
        for j in 1:size(x, 2)
            s = s + x[i, j] ^ 2
            x[i, j] = s
        end
    end
end
```

The `row_iter` function operates on the array in the first row, while the `col_iter` function operates on the array in the first column. We expect, based on the description of the previous array storage, that the `col_iter` function would be considerably faster than the `row_iter` function. Running the benchmarks, this is indeed what we see, as follows:

```
julia> a = rand(1000, 1000);

julia> @btime col_iter($a)
  1.116 ms (0 allocations: 0 bytes)

julia> @btime row_iter($a)
  3.429 ms (0 allocations: 0 bytes)
```

The difference between the two is quite significant. The column major access is more than twice as fast. This kind of difference in the inner loop of an algorithm can make a very noticeable difference in the overall runtime of a program. It is, therefore, crucial to consider the order in which multidimensional arrays are processed when writing performance-sensitive code.

Adjoints

Sometimes, you may have an algorithm that is naturally expressed as row-first. Converting the algorithm to column-first iteration can be a difficult process, prone to errors. In such cases, Julia provides an `Adjoint` type that can store a transpose of a matrix as a view into the original matrix. Row-wise iteration will be the fast option. We illustrate this in the following code.

```
julia> b=a'
1000×1000 LinearAlgebra.Adjoint{Float64,Array{Float64,2}}:
...

julia> @btime col_iter($b)
  3.521 ms (0 allocations: 0 bytes)

julia> @btime row_iter($b)
  1.160 ms (0 allocations: 0 bytes)
```

We see here that the timings of the function have been inverted from those in the previous section. Column iteration is now slower than row iteration. You will also notice that the time for row iteration is now the same as the column iteration was previously. This implies that using an `Adjoint` has no performance overhead at all.

Array initialization

Creating a new array is a two-step process. In step one, memory for the array needs to be allocated. The size of the memory is a product of the length of the array and the size of each element of the array (ignoring the small overhead of the type tag at the top). Second, the allocated memory needs to be filled with initial values. The simplest way to create arrays in Julia is by using the `fill` function, which does both these operations in one function, as shown in the following code:

```
julia> a = fill(1, 4, 4)
4×4 Array{Int64,2}:
 1 1 1 1
 1 1 1 1
 1 1 1 1
 1 1 1 1
```

Using `fill` in this way is not only convenient but also safer, since the memory that is returned to the program is filled with known good values. However, the operation to fill the memory is also expensive. For a performance-critical method to create arrays, the constructor can be called with a special `undef` keyword. In this case, memory is allocated, but not filled. This will be much faster, as we show in the following code that tries to create a 1,000 x 1,000 array of integers:

```
julia> @btime fill(1, 1000, 1000);
  1.142 ms (2 allocations: 7.63 MiB)

julia> @btime Array{Int64}(undef, 1000, 1000);
  131.204 µs (2 allocations: 7.63 MiB)
```

However, this is not without its downsides. For bitstypes (such as integers and floats), the array elements will contain random values that just happen to be present in that memory location. This could cause security issues if, for example, a buffer overflow is found in the runtime.

As shown in the following code, for reference types (strings or any composite type), accessing an uninitialized element will throw an `UndefRefError`:

```
julia> a=Array{Int}(undef, 2, 2)
2×2 Array{Int64,2}:
 4708348080  4567244464
 4768516416  4768514624

julia> b=Array{String}(undef, 2, 2)
2×2 Array{String,2}:
 #undef  #undef
 #undef  #undef

julia> b[1,1]
ERROR: UndefRefError: access to undefined reference
Stacktrace:
 [1] getindex(::Array{String,2}, ::Int64, ::Int64) at ./array.jl:730
 [2] top-level scope at none:0
```

As you can see in the previous code, when we ask for the first element of the `b` array, which has been initialized to undefined values, we get the `UndefRefError` exception.

Bounds checking

Like most modern dynamic languages, the Julia runtime performs bounds checks on arrays by default. This means that the Julia compiler and runtime verify that the arrays are not indexed outside their limits and that all the indexes lie between the actual start and end of an array. Reading values of memory mistakenly beyond the end of an array is often the cause of many bugs and security issues in unmanaged software. Hence, bounds checking is an important determinant of safety in your programs.

Removing the cost of bounds checking

However, as with any extra operation, bound checking has costs too. There are extra operations for all array reads and writes. While this cost is reasonably small and it is usually a good trade-off for safety, in some situations where it can be guaranteed that the array bounds are never crossed, it may be worthwhile to remove these checks. This is possible in Julia using the @inbounds macro as follows:

```
function prefix_bounds(a, b)
    for i in 2:size(a, 1)
        a[i] = b[i-1] + b[i]
    end
end

function prefix_inbounds(a, b)
    @inbounds for i in 2:size(a, 1)
        a[i] = b[i-1] + b[i]
    end
end
```

The @inbounds macro can be applied in front of a function or loop definition. Once this is done, all bound checking is disabled within the code block annotated with this macro. The performance benefit of doing this is small in absolute terms, but may be significant overall for hot inner loops. We measure this performance in the following code:

```
julia> a=zeros(Float64, 1000);

julia> b=rand(1000);

julia> @btime prefix_bounds($a, $b)
  925.303 ns (0 allocations: 0 bytes)

julia> @btime prefix_inbounds($a, $b)
  199.877 ns (0 allocations: 0 bytes)
```

The `@inbounds` annotation should only be used when it can be guaranteed that the array access within the annotated block will never be out of bounds. Usually, that means you should use this behavior only when the limits of the loop depend directly on the length of the array—in other words, for code in the form of `for i in 1:length(array)`. If you disable bound checking for some code and the array access is actually out of bounds, the results will be undefined. At best, the program will crash quickly.

Configuring bound checks at startup

The Julia runtime can use a command-line flag to set up bound-checking behavior for the entire session. The `-check-bounds` option can take two values: `yes` and `no`. These options will override any macro annotation in the source code.

When the Julia environment is started with `-check-bounds=yes`, all `@inbounds` annotations in the code are ignored, and bound checks are mandatorily performed. This option is useful when running tests to ensure that any code errors are properly reported and debugged.

Alternatively, when the Julia runtime is started with `-check-bounds=no`, no bound checking is done at all. This is equivalent to annotating all array access with the `@inbounds` macro. This option should only be used sparingly in the case of extremely performance-sensitive code, in which the system is very well tested and with minimal user inputs.

Allocations and in-place operations

Consider the following trivial function, `xpow`, which takes an integer as input and returns the first few powers of the number. Another function, `xpow_loop`, uses the first function to compute the sum of squares of a large sequence of numbers as follows:

```
function xpow(x)
    return [x x^2 x^3 x^4]
end

function xpow_loop(n)
    s = 0
    for i = 1:n
        s = s + xpow(i)[2]
    end
    return s
end
```

Benchmarking this function for large input shows that this function is quite slow:

```
julia> @btime xpow_loop($1000000)
   100.594 ms (4999441 allocations: 167.84 MiB)
```

The clue is in the number of allocations displayed in the preceding output. Within the xpow function, a four-element array is allocated for each invocation of this function. This allocation and the subsequent garbage collection take a significant amount of time. The number (and size) of allocations displayed in the preceding code snippet also hints at this problem.

Preallocating function output

You'll notice that in the xpow_loop function, we only require one array at a time to compute our result. The array returned from one xpow call is differenced in the next iteration of the loop. This suggests that all these allocations for the new array are a waste, and it may be easier to preallocate a single array to hold the result for each iteration as follows:

```
function xpow!(result::Array{Int, 1}, x)
    @assert length(result) == 4
    result[1] = x
    result[2] = x^2
    result[3] = x^3
    result[4] = x^4
end

function xpow_loop_noalloc(n)
    r = [0, 0, 0, 0]
    s = 0
    for i = 1:n
        xpow!(r, i)
        s = s + r[2]
    end
    s
end
```

Note that the xpow! function now has an exclamation mark in its name. This is a Julia convention that denotes that this function takes a variable that mutates as an argument. We allocate a single array outside the loop in the xpow_loop_noalloc function and then use it in all loop iterations to store the result of the xpow! function.

Take a look at the following code:

```
julia> @btime xpow_loop_noalloc($1000000)
  9.761 ms (1 allocation: 112 bytes)
```

The result of this change is quite impressive. The runtime of the function, doing the same computation as before, decreased by an order of magnitude. Even more impressively, instead of millions of allocations, the program got by with only a single allocation.

The message, then, is simple—pay attention to what allocations happen within your inner loops. Julia provides you with simple tools to track this, so this is easy to fix. In fact, we don't need a full-fledged benchmarking infrastructure to figure this out. The simple @time macro also displays the allocations clearly, as shown by the following code:

```
julia> @time xpow_loop(1_000_000)
  0.136251 seconds (4.00 M allocations: 152.580 MiB, 5.15% gc time)
333333833333500000

julia> @time xpow_loop_noalloc(1_000_000)
  0.010477 seconds (6 allocations: 288 bytes)
333333833333500000
```

sizehint!

One-dimensional arrays in Julia can be used as a dynamically sized list. In other words, you can push additional elements into an already allocated array. This is very convenient to program with, but the memory allocated to the array has to be expanded step by step at runtime, which can have some overhead. The sizehint! method allows the programmer to specify the eventual size of the dynamically resized collection. This method can also be used on other resizable collections, such as dictionaries.

Modern versions of Julia are actually very fast at allocating and resizing arrays, so this method is not really essential anymore. But it's good to keep in mind in case you find resizing arrays causes a bottleneck in your code.

Mutating functions

Given what we discussed in the previous section about the benefits of preallocating output, it should come as no surprise that many base library functions in Julia have mutating counterparts that modify their arguments, rather than allocating a new output structure.

For example, the `sort` base library function that sorts an array, allocates a new array of the same size as its input to hold its output—the sorted array. On the other hand, `sort!` makes an in-place sorting operation, in which the input array is itself sorted as follows:

```
julia> @btime sort(a);
  16.740 µs (1 allocation: 7.94 KiB)

julia> @btime sort!(a);
  5.757 µs (0 allocations: 0 bytes)
```

In this case, not only is the performance difference significant, but the allocating version of the function also allocates a large amount of memory.

Broadcasting

I hope that in your explorations of Julia, you have come across array broadcasting. This is the ability to perform an operation on each element of an array, rather than on the array as a whole, such as computing the square root of every element of a vector, as shown in the following code:

```
julia> a=collect(1:4);

julia> sqrt.(a)
4-element Array{Float64,1}:
 1.0
 1.4142135623730951
 1.7320508075688772
 2.0
```

More generally, it allows operations between arrays of different shapes, such as adding a vector to every column in a matrix, as follows:

```
julia> b=reshape(1:8, 4, 2)
4×2 reshape(::UnitRange{Int64}, 4, 2) with eltype Int64:
 1  5
 2  6
 3  7
 4  8

julia> b .+ a
4×2 Array{Int64,2}:
 2   6
 4   8
 6  10
 8  12
```

For the most part, broadcasting is a great syntactic feature in Julia, which makes it very easy and consistent to work with multidimensional arrays. In particular, unlike many other scientific computing languages, writing vectorized code in Julia is not a performance optimization. Writing loops in Julia, unlike say NumPy or Matlab, is pretty fast.

Even in vectorized languages, there is a downside to operating on vectors—combined operations do not compose efficiently. For example, for a vector `a`, the `b=sin.(cos.(a))` operation will usually compile to something like `temp=cos.(a)`, `Y=sin.(temp)`. This code has two problems: one, a temporary `temp` array is allocated, which is a problem for large input arrays, and gets worse as the length of the function chain increases; second, there are two loops through the elements of `a`.

In Julia, however, code like this will compile down to a single loop, with no temporary array allocated. The compiled code will look conceptually similar to the following code:

```
a=rand(10)
b = similar(a)
for i in 1:length(a)
    b[i] = sin(cos(a[i]))
end
```

This functionality, called loop fusion, is syntactically guaranteed. It is not a traditional best effort compiler optimization—it is guaranteed by the initial lowering pass of the compiler. Hence, for chains of function calls on arrays, broadcasting is highly recommended, not only for its elegance, but also for its performance benefits.

Finally, broadcasting can also help with preallocated output using the dotted assignment operator, `.=`. This allows the use of preallocated output with loop fusion, avoiding any extra copying.

In the following code, we reuse the preallocated `b` array, without any copying or additional looping:

```
julia> a = collect(1:10);

julia> b = fill(0.0, 10);

julia> b .= cos.(sin.(a))
10-element Array{Float64,1}:
 0.6663667453928805
 ...
```

We can verify that using the .= operator results in reduced allocations, and hence much quicker execution, as shown in the following code:

```julia
julia> @time b .= cos.(sin.(a));
  0.000013 seconds (8 allocations: 224 bytes)

julia> @btime c = cos.(sin.(a));
  0.026141 seconds (43.53 k allocations: 2.146 MiB)
```

Array views

Julia, similarly to most scientific languages, has a very convenient syntax for array slicing. Consider the following example that sums each column of a two-dimensional matrix. First, we will define a function that sums the elements of a vector to produce a scalar. We will then use this function inside a loop to sum the columns of a matrix, passing each column one by one to our vector adder as follows:

```julia
function sum_vector(x::Array{Float64, 1})
    s = zero(eltype(x))
    for i in 1:length(x)
        s = s + x[i]
    end
    return s
end

function sum_cols_matrix(x::Array{Float64, 2})
    num_cols = size(x, 2)
    s = zeros(num_cols)
    for i = 1:num_cols
        s[i] = sum_vector(x[:, i])
    end
    return s
end
```

The x[:, j] syntax denotes all the row elements of the jth column. In other words, it slices a matrix into its individual columns. Benchmarking this function, we will notice that the allocations and **garbage collection (GC)** times are quite high. Take a look at the following code:

```julia
julia> a = rand(1000, 1000);

julia> @benchmark sum_cols_matrix($a)
BenchmarkTools.Trial:
  memory estimate: 7.76 MiB
  allocs estimate: 1001
  --------------
  minimum time: 2.334 ms (0.00% GC)
  median time: 2.809 ms (0.00% GC)
  mean time: 3.331 ms (20.53% GC)
  maximum time: 53.357 ms (95.02% GC)
  --------------
  samples: 1495
  evals/sample: 1
```

The reason for the high allocation is the fact that, in Julia, array slices create a copy of the slice. In other words, for every x[:, j] data operation in the preceding code snippet, a new vector is allocated to hold the column, and the element values are copied into it from the original matrix. This obviously causes a large overhead in these kinds of algorithms. What we would like in this case is to create a vector representing one column of the matrix that shares its storage with the original array. This saves a significant amount of allocation and copying.

Julia includes a @view macro that allows us to slice arrays without copying the underlying data. This macro can be applied to any array indexing operation, wherein it returns a SubArray instance that is a view into the original array, rather than creating and copying a slice. Creating a SubArray is very fast, much faster than creating a sliced copy. Accessing a SubArray can be slower than accessing a regular dense array, but Julia's standard library has some extremely well-tuned code for this purpose. This code achieves performance nearly on par using regular arrays.

Using `@view`, we can rewrite our `sum_cols_matrix` function to reduce the allocations due to slicing. However, first, we need to loosen the parameter type of `sum_vector`, as we will now pass `SubArray` to this function. The `SubArray` type is a subtype of `AbstractArray`, but it is obviously a different type than the `Array` concrete type, which denotes dense, contiguous stored arrays. Take a look at the following code:

```
function sum_vector(x::AbstractArray)
    s = zero(eltype(x))
    for i in 1:length(x)
        s = s + x[i]
    end
    return s
end

function sum_cols_matrix_views(x::Array{Float64, 2})
    num_cols = size(x, 2); num_rows = size(x, 1)
    s = zeros(num_cols)
    for i = 1:num_cols
        s[i] = sum_vector(@view(x[:, i]))
    end
    return s
end
```

We can see that this function, which uses the views of arrays to operate on portions of it, is significantly faster than using slices and copies. More importantly, in the following benchmark, the number of allocations and memory used is many orders of magnitude lower than what we saw before:

```
julia> @benchmark sum_cols_matrix_views($a)
BenchmarkTools.Trial:
  memory estimate: 7.94 KiB
  allocs estimate: 1
  --------------
  minimum time: 1.100 ms (0.00% GC)
  median time: 1.137 ms (0.00% GC)
  mean time: 1.231 ms (0.00% GC)
  maximum time: 5.054 ms (0.00% GC)
  --------------
  samples: 4005
  evals/sample: 1
```

With views, we allocate about 7KiB for this operation, while we allocated over 7MiB when operating over the full array.

SIMD parallelization (AVX2, AVX512)

Single Instruction, Multiple Data (SIMD) is method of parallelizing computation within the CPU, whereby a single operation is performed on many data elements simultaneously. Modern CPU architectures contain instruction sets that can do this, operating on many variables at once.

On Intel processors, these types of instructions have been progressively implemented using names such as SSE, AVX2, and AVX512. Each of these implementations add on extra functionality, but also allow operations on wider data. SIMD was first implemented in older Intel processors, with the name SSE, which went through multiple versions. Most Intel and AMD processors from the last decade implement the AVX2 instruction set, which provides 256 bits of parallelism. More recent processors have an upgraded instruction set called AVX512, which, as the name suggests, can operate on 512 bits of data in one instruction. In other words, the amount of parallelization is larger in the later implementations.

Say you want to add two vectors, placing the result in a third vector. Let's imagine that there is no standard library function to achieve this, and you were writing a naïve implementation of this operation. Execute the following code:

```
function sum_vectors!(x, y, z)
    n = length(x)
    for i in 1:n
        x[i] = y[i] + z[i]
    end
end
```

Say the input arrays to this function has 1,000 elements. Then, the function essentially performs 1,000 sequential additions. A typical SIMD-enabled processor, however, can add up to eight numbers in one CPU cycle. Adding each of the elements sequentially can, therefore, be a waste of CPU capabilities.

On the other hand, rewriting code to operate on parts of the array in parallel can get complex quickly. Doing this for a wide range of algorithms can be an impossible task. Julia, as you would expect, makes this significantly easier using the `@simd` macro. Placing this macro against a loop gives the compiler the freedom to use SIMD instructions for the operations within this loop if possible, as shown in the following code:

```
function sum_vectors_simd!(x, y, z)
    n = length(x)
    @inbounds @simd for i = 1:n
        x[i] = y[i] + z[i]
    end
end
```

With this single change to the function, we can now achieve a significant performance gain on this operation, as follows:

```
a = zeros(Float32, 1_000_000);
b = rand(Float32, 1_000_000);
c = rand(Float32, 1_000_000)

julia> @btime sum_vectors!($a, $b, $c)
  1.130 ms (0 allocations: 0 bytes)

julia> @btime sum_vectors_simd!($a, $b, $c)
  932.636 µs (0 allocations: 0 bytes)
```

There are a few limitations to using the `@simd` macro. This does not make every loop faster. In particular, note that using SIMD implies that the order of operations within and across the loop might change. The compiler needs to be certain that the reordering will be safe before it attempts to parallelize a loop. Therefore, before adding a `@simd` annotation to your code, you need to ensure that the loop has the following properties:

- Each iteration of the loop is independent of the others. That is, no iteration of the loop uses a value from a previous iteration or waits for its completion. The significant exception to this rule is that certain reductions are permitted.
- The arrays being operated upon within the loop do not overlap in memory.

- The loop body is straight-line code without branches or function calls.
- The number of iterations of the loop is obvious. In practical terms, this means that the loop should typically be expressed on the length of the arrays within it.
- The subscript (or index variable) within the loop changes by one for each iteration. In other words, the subscript is unit stride.
- Bounds checking is disabled for SIMD loops. (Bound checking can cause branches due to exceptional conditions.)

To check whether the compiler successfully vectorized your code, use the `@code_llvm` macro to inspect the generated LLVM bitcode. While the output might be long and inscrutable, the keywords to look for in the output are sections prefixed with `vector` and vectorized operations that look similar to `<n * float>`.

The following is an extract from the output of `@code_llvm` for the function we ran before, showing a successful vectorization of the operations. Thus, we know that the performance gains we observed are indeed coming from an automatic vectorization of our sequential code:

```
julia> @code_llvm sum_vectors_simd!(a, b, c)
....
%28 = getelementptr inbounds float, float addrspace(13)* %22, i64 %index
    %29 = bitcast float addrspace(13)* %28 to <8 x float> addrspace(13)*
    %wide.load = load <8 x float>, <8 x float> addrspace(13)* %29, align 4
    %30 = getelementptr float, float addrspace(13)* %28, i64 8
    %31 = bitcast float addrspace(13)* %30 to <8 x float> addrspace(13)*
    %wide.load23 = load <8 x float>, <8 x float> addrspace(13)* %31, align
4
```

Alternatively, you can inspect the generated assembly code using `@code_native`, and look for vector instructions in the output:

```
julia> @code_native sum_vectors_simd!(a, b, c)
....
  vaddps (%edx,%ecx,4), %ymm0, %ymm0
  vaddps 32(%edx,%ecx,4), %ymm1, %ymm1
  vaddps 64(%edx,%ecx,4), %ymm2, %ymm2
  vaddps 96(%edx,%ecx,4), %ymm3, %ymm3
```

Like most other output in this book, this code has been run on my laptop that happens to contain an Intel i5-4258U CPU, which implements AVX2 instructions, and operates on 256 bits (32 bytes) of data in one operation.

When this is run on a larger server with a more modern processor (such as a Xeon 4114), which is capable of AVX512, the generated code is different, as we see below:

```
julia> @code_native sum_vectors_simd!(a, b, c)
....
  vaddps (%rdx,%rcx,4), %zmm0, %zmm0
  vaddps 64(%rdx,%rcx,4), %zmm1, %zmm1
  vaddps 128(%rdx,%rcx,4), %zmm2, %zmm2
  vaddps 192(%rdx,%rcx,4), %zmm3, %zmm3
```

You will notice that the assembly code operates on data twice as wide as before. The offsets now are 512 bits (64 bytes) wide. In other words, this processor allows double the amount of parallelism compared to my laptop.

SIMD.jl

The @simd macro we saw previously is only a hint to the compiler, it does not guarantee that SIMD operations are used on the CPU. And in some cases, LLVM might be able to generate SIMD parallel code even without any external hints. However, even with the annotation, often regular, a non-parallel code may be generated, which could be either due to a limitation of the compiler or because the code is inherently non-parallel.

In situations where, as a programmer, you want to be absolutely certain that some operations are implemented as SIMD instructions, the SIMD.jl package provides low-level types and functions that allow you to specify this. Most applications honestly do not need this level of intervention, but when you do need this, Julia makes it (relatively) easy. This package can be installed via the package manager is the usual way.

As we described previously, SIMD allows the processor to apply an operation to multiple values in one instruction. Thus, it should not be a surprise that the primary type in this package is a fixed length vector, Vec{N, T}, which is parameterized by its length and its underlying type. For example, a = Vec{4, Int64}(1) creates a vector of 4 Int64s, all of which have the value of 1. The length of the vector should match the length of the size of the SIMD registers on your machine. In the following example, I use 4 Int64 or Float64 values, since my CPU uses AVX2, which has a vector size of 256.

The simplest use of these types is to use the built-in reduction functions. The following are defined in the package: `all`, `any`, `maximum`, `minimum`, `sum`, and `prod`, as follows:

```
julia> using SIMD

julia> a=Vec{4, Float64}((1.0, 2.0, 3.0, 4.0))
<4 x Float64>[1.0, 2.0, 3.0, 4.0]

julia> @btime sum($a)
  1.761 ns (0 allocations: 0 bytes)
10.0
```

We can verify the use of parallel operations by inspecting the generated code. We can see that the following code has no loop; instead, a small number of vector (meaning parallel) operation is all it takes:

```
julia> @code_native sum(a)
    vmovupd (%edi), %ymm0
    vextractf128 $1, %ymm0, %xmm1
    vaddpd %xmm1, %xmm0, %xmm0
    vpermilpd $1, %xmm0, %xmm1 ## xmm1 = xmm0[1,0]
    vaddsd %xmm1, %xmm0, %xmm0
    vzeroupper
    retl
    nopl (%eax)
```

We can also verify that summing a vector of this size using regular add operations takes significantly longer, as shown here:

```
function naive_sum(x::Vector{Float64})
    s = 0.0
    for i=1:length(x)
        s=s+x[i]
    end
    return s
end

julia> b=[1.,2.,3.,4.]
4-element Array{Float64,1}:
 1.0
 2.0
 3.0
 4.0

julia> @btime naive_sum($b)
  3.829 ns (0 allocations: 0 bytes)
10.0
```

As you saw in the SIMD-compiled function, the processor can work on four values together. If you have a longer array, you will then have to create blocks of four numbers to process using this mechanism. Working at this low level, therefore, is somewhat tedious, but sometimes necessary. We will not dwell too much on how to write such kernels, but we will leave you with one example of writing a SIMD-enabled function to add two arrays, taken from the `SIMD.jl` documentation as follows:

```
function vadd!(xs::Vector{T}, ys::Vector{T}, ::Type{Vec{N,T}}) where {N, T}
    @assert length(ys) == length(xs)
    @assert length(xs) % N == 0
    lane = VecRange{N}(0)
    @inbounds for i in 1:N:length(xs)
        xs[lane + i] += ys[lane + i]
    end
end
```

In this function, we pass the SIMD type we want to operate on as a parameter to make it easier to write. Inside the function, we split the array into blocks of the correct size (`i in 1:N:length(xs)`), and add the elements of the block. The indexing operation by the `VecRange` will convert the regular Julia array that is passed into the SIMD specific `Vec` type, which in turn will force the compiler to use the SIMD operations for the addition.

Specialized array types

The flexibility of Julia's type system, along with multiple dispatches, makes it easy to write code that is specialized for particular domains or situations. We've seen earlier how Julia's compiler will compile separate methods for different input types. So, for example, different methods may be compiled for adding integers or floats. But the real power comes in using the same principles in third-party libraries, or indeed, your own code.

Static arrays

Julia's arrays are very powerful and can be used in a whole range of use cases. They can be used as mathematical constructs or containers of arbitrary objects. Operations on arrays are usually highly optimized. However, in situations where the size of an array is small and known exactly by the programmer, certain additional optimizations may be available. For example, points in a 3D space may be represented by a vector with a length of three. Or, a pixel in an image may be represented as a vector with a length of four (red-green-blue-transparency).

In these cases, and others, knowing the size of arrays upfront can lead to much more efficient code. The StaticArrays.jl package allows programmers to write code with fixed-size arrays in order to enable these optimizations.

These optimizations can be quite significant. According to the package documentation, your code may speed up from 3 to 100 times by the use of StaticArrays. I would, therefore, recommend that you consider using StaticArrays rather than regular arrays if your problem consists of many small vectors of fixed sizes. A general heuristic is that StaticArrays are useful for arrays of up to 100 elements.

Like all Julia packages, StaticArrays can be installed via the Julia package manager as shown here:

```
julia> using Pkg

julia> Pkg.add("StaticArrays")
```

The package provides the SVector and SMatrix types, which are used for one and two-dimensional fixed size arrays, respectively. Furthermore, these types are immutable, in that the elements of the arrays cannot be changed after creation. Separate types are available when mutation is required: MVector and MMatrix. Finally, the SArray and MArray types are provided for multidimensional arrays.

These array types can be created via constructors or converted using a macro, as shown in the following code:

```
julia> using StaticArrays

julia> a=SVector(1, 2, 3, 4)
4-element SArray{Tuple{4},Int64,1,4}:
 1
 2
 3
 4

julia> b = @SVector [3, 4, 5, 6]
4-element SArray{Tuple{4},Int64,1,4}:
 3
 4
 5
 6
```

One crucial aspect of `StaticArrays` is that the size of the array is encoded in the type information. This implies that the length of the array is known at compile time, and this fact enables all the performance optimizations when using fixed sized arrays. To see how significant these optimizations can be, we measure the time to cross multiply the length-4 array with itself. First, to generate a baseline, we measure the speed of the operation on a regular array, as follows:

```
julia> c=[1,2,3,4];

julia> @btime $c*$c'
  87.867 ns (2 allocations: 224 bytes)
4×4 Array{Int64,2}:
 1  2  3   4
 2  4  6   8
 3  6  9  12
 4  8  12  16
```

Next, we run the same computation on a `SArray`, as shown here:

```
julia> @btime $a*$a'
  0.030 ns (0 allocations: 0 bytes)
4×4 SArray{Tuple{4,4},Int64,2,16}:
 1  2  3   4
 2  4  6   8
 3  6  9  12
 4  8  12  16
```

The time reported by this computation is unbelievably small—a fraction of a nanosecond. What has happened is that the compiler has been able to look into the benchmarking loop, and hoisted the constant result out, which it was able to compute at compile time. While the measurement, therefore, is probably invalid, this in itself probably shows some of the benefits of using `StaticArrays`, namely, that the compiler has much greater information about the computation, and can thus enable many more optimizations. You'll note that even though we run the same computation, the compiler has not been able to figure this out for regular arrays.

In any case, for pedagogical purposes, we can attempt to defeat this optimization by using a `Ref` value so that we can measure the actual time this code takes to run. A `Ref` is an indirect reference to a value, and using it forces a runtime dereference to get that value. In other words, the value itself is now hidden from the compiler.

As shown in the following code, using this trick, we now get a more reliable timing, which is still an order of magnitude faster than regular arrays:

```julia
julia> @btime $(Ref(a))[] * $(Ref(a'))[]
  9.349 ns (0 allocations: 0 bytes)
4×4 SArray{Tuple{4,4},Int64,2,16}:
 1  2   3   4
 2  4   6   8
 3  6   9  12
 4  8  12  16
```

It should be obvious, therefore, that `StaticArrays` can be of immense help in speeding up operations on small, fixed-size arrays.

Structs of arrays

Consider a complex number, which, as you know, consists of a real and imaginary part. In Julia (and indeed, most other languages), it is stored as a composite type—a struct that has two fields, `re` and `im` for the real and imaginary parts, respectively. Each of these fields are stored as the same number type, `Int64` or `Float64` typically, and together, they create the type `Complex`.

Now, consider an array of `Complex` numbers. With each `Complex` struct containing two numbers, the array would be laid out in this manner:

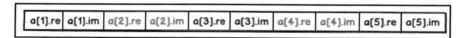

When operating on arrays on this type, the CPU pulls `re` and `im` one after the other. However, that kind of operation is not optimal to take advantage of SIMD parallelization in the CPU. As we've seen in the previously, the benefits of SIMD accrue really when the CPU can perform the same operations on homogeneous data. In other words, it would be the fastest to pull all the `re`s in together, and then pull in all the `im` entries. This can be achieved by storing the arrays in the following fashion:

| a[1].re | a[2].re | a[3].re | a[4].re | a[5].re | a[1].im | a[2].im | a[3].im | a[4].im | a[5].im |

In other words, instead of storing an array of structs of two integers, we store a struct with two arrays of integers. This is known as the **Struct of Arrays (SoA)** optimization. While this is not very difficult to store and process manually, we then lose the ability to use higher-level types such as the `Complex` type. We also lose the ability to use function dispatch on these types.

The `StructArrays` package allows us to have our cake and eat it too. We can create and store optimized structs of arrays, but get the individual structs back on indexing operations. As usual, the package can be installed via the Julia package manager.

`StructArrays` can be created by converting regular arrays of structs. Let's create an array of a million random complex numbers, and convert it to a `StructArray` as shown here:

```julia
julia> using StructArrays

julia> a=Complex.(rand(1000000), rand(1000000))
1000000-element Array{Complex{Float64},1}:
  0.2710739454715172 + 0.7493001957068579im
...

julia> b = StructArray(a)
1000000-element StructArray{Complex{Float64},1,NamedTuple{(:re,
:im),Tuple{Array{Float64,1},Array{Float64,1}}}}:
  0.2710739454715172 + 0.7493001957068579im
...
```

This, of course, causes a copy, and as a result, allocates double the memory. Alternative approaches include using an iterator or generator are also an option, as shown in the following code:

```julia
julia> c = StructArray(i + 2*i*im for i in 1:10)
10-element StructArray{Complex{Int64},1,NamedTuple{(:re,
:im),Tuple{Array{Int64,1},Array{Int64,1}}}}:
  1 + 2im
  2 + 4im
...
```

Or, as with regular arrays, an uninitialized `StructArray` might be created using `undef`, and then filled like so:

```julia
julia> d = StructArray{ComplexF64}(undef, 10)
10-element StructArray{Complex{Float64},1,NamedTuple{(:re,
:im),Tuple{Array{Float64,1},Array{Float64,1}}}}:
 2.3498567246e-314 + 2.3498567246e-314im
               0.0 + 0.0im
...
```

```
julia> using Random

julia> Random.rand!(d)
10-element StructArray{Complex{Float64},1,NamedTuple{(:re,
:im),Tuple{Array{Float64,1},Array{Float64,1}}}}:
    0.59703447425146 + 0.3765067723340896im
    0.9154630457422517 + 0.16780096637488895im
...
```

We can inspect that the StructArray stores each field of the struct as a separate
contiguous array. In other words, re and im are stored as separate arrays. Yet, indexing the
StructArray returns an object of the Complex type, as shown in the following code:

```
julia> d.re
10-element Array{Float64,1}:
 0.59703447425146
 0.9154630457422517
....

julia> d[5]
0.9213836758979468 + 0.7040669382497653im

julia> typeof(d[5])
Complex{Float64}
```

Having created the arrays, let's operate on them to verify their performance improvement
as follows:

```
function accum(x, z)
    s = zero(eltype(x))
    @simd for i in 1:length(x)
        @inbounds s += x[i] * z
    end
    s
end

julia> @btime accum($a, 1.5 + 2.5im)
  1.531 ms (0 allocations: 0 bytes)
-499158.1112726756 + 2.000721048164868e6im

julia> @btime accum($b, 1.5 + 2.5im)
  1.415 ms (0 allocations: 0 bytes)
-499158.1112726756 + 2.000721048164868e6im
```

We see a small but noticeable improvement in running the operation over `StructArrays`. As your operations get more complex, the benefits of using `StructArrays` will only increase.

Yeppp!

Many algorithms for scientific computing involve computing transcendental functions (`log`, `sin`, and `cos`) on arrays of floating point values. These are heavily used operations with strict correctness requirements, and thus, have been the target of many optimization efforts over the years. Faster versions of these functions can make a huge impact on the performance of many applications in the scientific computing domain.

In this area, the **Yeppp!** the software suite can be considered state of the art. Primarily written at Georgia Institute of Technology by Marat Dukhan, Yeppp! provides optimized implementations of modern processors of these functions, which are much faster compared to the implementations in system libraries.

Julia has a very easy-to-use binding to Yeppp! within a package. It can be installed using the built-in package management mechanism, `Pkg.add("Yeppp")`. Once installed, the functions are available with the `Yeppp` module. There is no simpler way to get a *4x* performance boost. With performance gains of this magnitude, there is little reason to use anything else for code where a large number of transcendental functions need to be computed. Run the following code:

```julia
julia> using Yeppp

julia> a=rand(1_000_000);

julia> @btime log.($a);
  8.683 ms (2 allocations: 7.63 MiB)

julia> @btime Yeppp.log($a)
  2.384 ms (2 allocations: 7.63 MiB)
```

`Yeppp` also provides in-place versions of its functions that can be faster in many situations, saving allocations and subsequent GC. The in-place version of `log`, for example, provides an almost *2x* performance gain over the allocating version we ran before. Take a look at the following code:

```julia
julia> @btime Yeppp.log!($a)
  1.862 ms (0 allocations: 0 bytes)
```

The `Yeppp` Julia package provides implementations of some common vectorized functions, including `log`, `sin`, `exp`, and `sumabs`. Refer to `https://github.com/JuliaLang/Yeppp.jl` for full details of its capabilities.

Writing generic library functions with arrays

The suggestions in the previous sections should make your array code fast and high performance. If you are directly writing code to solve your own problems, this should be enough. However, if you are writing library routines that may be called by other programs, you will need to heed additional concerns. Your function may be called with arrays of different kinds and with different dimensions. To write generic code that is fast with all custom types built-in, and for arrays of many dimensions, you need to be careful in how you iterate over the elements of the arrays.

All Julia arrays are subtypes of the `AbstractArray` type. All abstract arrays must provide facilities for indexation and iteration. However, these can be implemented very differently for different types of arrays. The default array is `DenseArray`, which stores its elements in contiguous memory. As discussed before, these elements can be pointers or values, but in either case, they are stored in contiguous memory. This means that linear indexing is very fast for all these arrays. However, this is not true for all kinds of arrays.

The term **linear indexing** refers to the ability to index a multidimensional array by a single scalar index. So, for example, if we have a three-dimensional array, x, with 10 elements in each dimension, it can be indexed with a single integer in the range of 1 to 1,000. In other words, $x[1], x[2], ...x[10], x[11], ...x[99]$, and $x[100]$ are consecutive elements of the array.

As described earlier, Julia arrays are stored in a major order column, so linear indexing runs through the array in this order. This makes linear indexing particularly cache-friendly because contiguous memory segments are accessed consecutively. In contrast, **Cartesian indexing** uses the complete dimensions of the array to index it. The three-dimensional array x is indexed by three integers $x[i, j, k]$.

For example, subarrays can be efficiently indexed using Cartesian indexing, but linear indexing for subarrays is much slower due to the need to compute a division and a remainder for each indexing operation. While Cartesian indexing is useful when the number of dimensions of an array are known, generic code typically uses linear indexing to work with multidimensional arrays. This, then, may create performance pitfalls.

As an example of a function that can work with generic multidimensional arrays, let's write a simple function that sums all the elements in an array as follows:

```
function mysum_linear(a::AbstractArray)
    s=zero(eltype(a))
    for i in 1:length(a)
        s=s + a[i]
    end
    return s
end
```

This function works with arrays of any type and dimension. We verify this below, when we call it with a range, a three-dimensional array, a two-dimensional array, and a two-dimensional subarray, respectively:

```
julia> x = 1:1000000;

julia> mysum_linear(x)
500000500000

julia> mysum_linear(reshape(x, 100, 100, 100))
500000500000

julia> mysum_linear(reshape(x, 1000, 1000))
500000500000

julia> mysum_linear(@view reshape(x, 1000, 1000)[1:500, 1:500] )
62437625000
```

If we benchmark these functions, we will note that calling the same function on a subarray is significantly slower than calling it on a regular dense array as shown here:

```
julia> y = reshape(x, 1000, 1000);

julia> @btime mysum_linear($y)
  344.880 µs (0 allocations: 0 bytes)
500000500000

julia> @btime mysum_linear(@view $y[1:500, 1:500] )
  1.401 ms (0 allocations: 0 bytes)
62437625000
```

In situations like this where we want to write generic functions that can be performant with different kinds of arrays, the advice is to not use linear indexing. So, what should we use?

The simplest option is to directly iterate the array rather than iterating its indices. The iterator for each kind of array will choose the most optimal strategy for high performance. Hence, the code to add the elements of a multidimensional array can be written as follows:

```
function mysum_in(a::AbstractArray)
    s = zero(eltype(a))
    for i in a
        s = s + i
    end
end
```

If we benchmark this function, we can see the difference in performance, wherein the new function recovers all the performance when operating on a view, as shown here:

```
julia> @btime mysum_in(@view $y[1:500, 1:500])
  344.877 µs (0 allocations: 0 bytes)
```

This strategy is usable when the algorithm only requires the elements of the array and not its indexes. If the indexes need to be available within the loop, they can be written using the eachindex() method. Each array defines an optimized eachindex() method that allows the iteration of its index efficient. We can then rewrite the sum function as follows, even though for this particular function, we do not actually need indexes:

```
function mysum_eachindex(a::AbstractArray)
    s = zero(eltype(a))
    for i in eachindex(a)
        s = s + a[i]
    end
end
```

The benchmark numbers demonstrate an order-of-magnitude improvement in the speed of these functions when not using linear indexing for subarrays. Once again, the performance overhead of using a view has gone away, as shown here:

```
julia> @btime mysum_eachindex(@view $y[1:500, 1:500] )
  377.050 µs (0 allocations: 0 bytes)
```

Writing code in this manner, therefore, allows our function to be used correctly and efficiently by all manner of arrays in Julia.

Summary

In this chapter, we covered the performance characteristics in Julia of the most important data structure in scientific computing—the array. We discussed why Julia's design enables extremely fast array operations and how to get the best performance in our code when operating on arrays. This brings us to the end of our journey of creating the fastest possible code in Julia. Using all the tips discussed until now, the performance of your code should approach that of well-written C.

Sometimes, however, this isn't enough, and we want higher performance; our data may be larger or our computations intensive. In this case, the only option is to parallelize our processing using multiple CPUs and systems. In the next chapter, we will take a brief look at the features that Julia provides to write parallel systems easily.

Accelerating Code with the GPU

7

Accelerator cards for display graphics have a long and storied past. They've been available since the 70s. The late 90s, however, saw the introduction of programmable shaders that allowed the display to be generated by little programs that ran on specialized chips. It was quickly apparent, however, that the code used to draw triangles on screen, and transform and light them, could be generalized to many other fields.

Originally designed for fast graphics calculations, they have found use in accelerating many kinds of numerical code. The defining characteristic of these processors has been their ability to run many threads—in the order of hundreds or thousands—in parallel, which then allows significant speedups in algorithms that can take advantage of this facility. Therefore, the general-purpose **Graphics Processing Unit** (**GPU**) has turned out to be one of the best ways of running fast parallel computations. Its applications in deep learning have been particularly influential and important.

In this chapter, we will see how to write Julia code that takes advantage of modern GPUs. Unlike most other languages, using the GPU from Julia is not just about calling out to pre-built C libraries; we are able to compile Julia code directly to the GPU. Of course, Julia's easy-to-use C-interop means calling existing GPU libraries, such as **CUDA® Deep Neural Network library** (**cuDNN**) (for deep learning primitives on the GPU) is trivial, but it is in writing your own kernels that run directly in the GPU that you can see the power of Julia in this area.

After reading this chapter, you should be able to use GPU-enabled packages, and also be able to write simple GPU kernels yourself. In particular, we will discuss the following topics:

- Getting started with GPUs
- CUDA, PTX and its use from Julia

- CuArrays - Arrays on the GPU
- Analyzing the performance of GPU code

Technical requirements

This chapter requires a basic familiarity with the concepts of heterogeneous computing on the GPU. The code here also assumes access to an NVIDIA GPU built within the last five years or so. So, additional software also needs to be installed beyond Julia (such as the CUDA toolkit), but we show you how to do that within the chapter. Also, while everything else in this book is operating system agnostic and should run in all platforms where Julia is supported, the code in this chapter is tested only on the Linux operating system, and may not work in the same way on other operating systems.

Getting started with GPUs

To begin, you'll need a computer with a discrete GPU installed. For the purposes of this chapter, that will mean a GPU manufactured by NVIDIA. While other brands of GPUs are available, support for those is much weaker, both for general scientific programs, and, in particular, in Julia. Hence, we will not have the opportunity to discuss them in this chapter and we limit our focus to NVIDIA GPUs.

Once you have access to a computer with a GPU (whether on your desktop or on the cloud), the first order of business is to install a driver and CUDA toolkit on the machine. The exact instructions will depend on your operating system and the GPU model you use. You will need to ensure that the versions of the device driver and CUDA toolkit are compatible.

 CUDA is the programming model used by NVIDIA for general-purpose computing on its GPUs. It's typically programmed in C++ (with certain extensions) and compiled by the *nvcc* compiler. It's a proprietary technology that is used only with NVIDIA GPUs. AMD devices use a more open programming platform known as OpenCL, but CUDA and NVIDIA are, by far, the market leaders in this area.

Once installed, you can check the presence and status of the GPU using the `nvidia-smi` command that comes with the CUDA toolkit, as shown in the following screenshot:

```
jrun@notebook-jg7xj:/home/jrun$ nvidia-smi
Mon May 20 22:16:40 2019
+-----------------------------------------------------------------------------+
| NVIDIA-SMI 396.26                 Driver Version: 396.26                    |
|-------------------------------+----------------------+----------------------+
| GPU  Name            Persistence-M| Bus-Id        Disp.A | Volatile Uncorr. ECC |
| Fan  Temp  Perf  Pwr:Usage/Cap|          Memory-Usage | GPU-Util  Compute M. |
|===============================+======================+======================|
|   0  Tesla K80            Off | 0000D718:00:00.0 Off |                    0 |
| N/A   51C    P0    87W / 149W |   9222MiB / 11441MiB |     93%      Default |
+-------------------------------+----------------------+----------------------+

+-----------------------------------------------------------------------------+
| Processes:                                                       GPU Memory |
|  GPU       PID   Type   Process name                             Usage      |
|=============================================================================|
+-----------------------------------------------------------------------------+
jrun@notebook-jg7xj:/home/jrun$ ▮
```

This output shows that I have an NVIDIA Tesla K80 GPU on my machine, with about 12 GB of onboard memory.

> The GPU name in my machine is Tesla K80. Tesla is the brand name used for server class, general-purpose GPUs by NVIDIA. These devices, though descended from graphics cards, usually do not have the capability of graphical output.

> The **K** in K80 refers to the **Kepler** microarchitecture. Subsequent microarchitectures, present in later and more advanced devices, are the *Pascal* (for example, the P100) and then the *Volta* (for example, the V100). The next set of devices, released in 2019, will be built on the Turing microarchitecture.

> Consumer or desktop GPUs are branded GeForce and Titan (with sub-brands of GTX and RTX for higher performance units). While based on the same set of microarchitectures, they are more suited for graphics and gaming. However, they are equally useful for computational tasks.

In order to use the GPU effectively, it's useful to understand how the GPU works, and what it is optimized for. One mental model that may be applied is to think of a GPU as being a computer on its own with hundreds or thousands of processor cores. The cores can all run simultaneously, performing the same operations on multiple data points in one cycle. It is important to note that each individual operation might be very slow, but it's the parallelism that makes it fast.

Moreover, a GPU has its own memory, and its cores can operate only on data within that memory. Thus, GPU programs can spend a significant amount of time in copying data from and to the main (CPU) memory to the GPU memory. Programming GPUs therefore needs special considerations in terms of the design and architecture of your programs. You need to write the compute as vectorized operations, and be careful in how (and how often) data is copied from the CPU and GPU. However, Julia can make it easy for a set of many operations, where all you need to do is use broadcasting to make things parallel.

CUDA and Julia

The majority of the functionality for working with NVIDIA GPUs is contained in two Julia packages: CUDAnative and CuArrays. Both these packages can be installed using Julia's package manager. We also install the CUDAdrv package, which contains some tooling that we will use later, as shown in the following code:

```
julia> using Pkg

julia> Pkg.add("CUDAnative");

julia> Pkg.add("CuArrays");

julia> Pkg.add("CUDAdrv");
```

CUDAnative contains the basic building blocks of interfacing Julia code with the GPU. To see it in use, let's write the simplest possible function, printing a number, but executed on the GPU like so:

```
using CUDAnative
function cudaprint(n)
    @cuprintf("Thread %ld prints: %ld\n",
        threadIdx().x, n)
    return
end
```

This is a regular Julia function, even though it uses some GPU-specific invocations. We can then run this function on the GPU via the @cuda macro, specifying the number of threads that should be used as follows:

```
julia> @cuda threads=4 cudaprint(10)
Thread 1 prints: 10
Thread 2 prints: 10
Thread 3 prints: 10
Thread 4 prints: 10
```

The package also provides introspection facilities to view the generated code that is actually run on the device, similar to the `@code_*` macros we've seen before:

```
julia> @device_code_ptx @cuda cudaprint(10)
...
  mov.u64 %SPL, __local_depot0;
  cvta.local.u64 %SP, %SPL;
  ld.param.u64 %rd1, [ptxcall_cudaprint_1_param_0];
  mov.u64 %rd2, __unnamed_1;
  cvta.global.u64 %rd3, %rd2;
  add.u64 %rd4, %SP, 0;
  add.u64 %rd5, %SPL, 0;
  mov.u32 %r1, %tid.x;
  add.s32 %r2, %r1, 1;
  cvt.u64.u32 %rd6, %r2;
  st.local.u64 [%rd5], %rd6;
  st.local.u64 [%rd5+8], %rd1;
...
```

NVIDIA uses a pseudo-assembly intermediate language known as **Parallel Thread Execution (PTX)**. We generate PTX from Julia code using the LLVM PTX compiler backend. Once generated, the PTX is converted to binary code by a compiler built into the device driver. This binary code can also be viewed using the `@device_code_sass` macro as follows:

```
julia> @device_code_sass @cuda cudaprint(10)
...
.text.ptxcall_cudaprint_22:
        MOV R1, c[0x0][0x44];
        S2R R0, SR_TID.X;
        ISUB R1, R1, 0x10;
        MOV R8, c[0x0][0x140];
        MOV R9, c[0x0][0x144];
        MOV R3, RZ;
        IADD R2, R0, 0x1;
        STL.64 [R1+0x8], R8;
        MOV32I R4, 32@lo(__unnamed_1);
        MOV32I R5, 32@hi(__unnamed_1);
        MOV R7, RZ;
        LOP.OR R6, R1, c[0x0][0x24];
        STL.64 [R1], R2;
        JCAL `(vprintf);
        MOV RZ, RZ;
        EXIT;
...
```

There are also `@device_code_lowered`, `@device_code_typed`, and `@device_code_warntype` macros, similar to the ones for the CPU that we've seen in the previous chapters. These macros show the code that runs on the GPU, in various states of compilation, as shown here:

```
julia> @device_code_lowered @cuda cudaprint(10)
Thread 1 prints: 10
1-element Array{Any,1}:
 CodeInfo(
1 ─ %1 = (Main.threadIdx)()
│   %2 = (Base.getproperty)(%1, :x)
│   %3 = (CUDAnative.promote_c_argument)(%2)
│   %4 = (CUDAnative.promote_c_argument)(n)
│        (CUDAnative._cuprintf)(Val{Symbol("Thread %ld prints: %ld\n")}(), %3, %4)
└──      return
)
```

Much more detail on this package is available on its documentation page at https://juliagpu.gitlab.io/CUDAnative.jl.

CuArrays

The `CuArrays` package is probably the most significant part of the GPU ecosystem in Julia. It provides an array type for storing data on the GPU and operating on it. Since GPU code needs to be vectorized, an array is the primary data type that needs to be used in all cases.

A `CuArray` datatype can be created by calling its constructor with a regular Julia array. Once created, GPU kernels may be called on it. The package includes kernels for basic mathematical operators, which are typically called via dot-broadcast. As with all broadcasts in Julia, the operations are fused, which means that on the GPU, a single fused kernel is run on the array, even though multiple operations exist on the source. In other words, the power, subtraction, multiplication, addition, and squaring in the following expression is all combined into a single block of processing:

```
julia> using CuArrays

julia> a=CuArray([1f0, 2f0, 3f0])
3-element CuArray{Float32,1}:
 1.0
 2.0
 3.0

julia> b = a.^2 .- a.*2 .+ sqrt.(a)
3-element CuArray{Float32,1}:
```

```
0.0
1.4142135
4.732051
```

TIP

1f0 is Julia shorthand for creating a 32-bit float, or a Float32. By default, a floating point number in Julia (such as 1.0) is 64-bit, also known as Float64. GPUs generally have faster operations on 32-bit numbers.

Monte Carlo simulation on the GPU

For another example, let's try to calculate the value of Pi using a Monte Carlo simulation. This is a simple algorithm, which is equivalent to throwing a dart onto a circle.

Consider a circle with a radius of one, enclosed within a square. We simulate the throwing of darts by generating two random numbers, x and y, both between zero and one. Since the numbers take values between zero and one, this can be interpreted as throwing the dart in the first quadrant of the circle. We check whether the position of the dart is inside the circle, which is true when $x^2 + y^2 <= 1$.

We then repeat this many times and count the number of times the point is within the circle. The probability of the dart falling within the circle will be equal to its area, which we denote by x. Our simulation runs in the first quadrant, so we multiply the ratio by four to get the area of the circle. Take the formula for the area of a circle, $a = \pi r^2$, and substitute the value of r, which is one. This implies $\pi = a = 4x$, which is the formula you see in the following code:

```
using CuArrays.CURAND

function pi_gpu(n)
    4 * sum(curand(Float64, n).^2 .+ curand(Float64, n).^2 .<= 1) / n
end
```

Note, once again, how the GPU code uses *broadcast*. The curand function will generate a set of n random numbers on the GPU (this creates a CuArray), and then all subsequent operations will occur on the GPU. The key point here is that the broadcasted operations (the squaring and the addition) happen in parallel across all the computation units on the GPU.

For comparison, we write the same algorithm to run on the CPU, but this time using a loop as follows:

```
function pi_serial(n)
    inside = 0
    for i in 1:n
        x, y = rand(), rand()
        inside += (x^2 + y^2 <= 1)
    end
    return 4 * inside / n
end
```

We benchmark both these implementations to see that the GPU, in this case, is at least an order of magnitude faster as regards this task, as shown in the following code:

```
julia> @btime pi_serial(10_000_000)
  36.189 ms (0 allocations: 0 bytes)
3.1410748

julia> @btime pi_gpu(10_000_000)
  2.675 ms (158 allocations: 6.02 KiB)
3.1419156
```

This very simple algorithm gives us a sense of the benefits of using the GPU.

Both the preceding CPU and GPU functions are using Float64 values for the computation. Let's define a version of the function using Float32 values, as shown here:

```
function pi_gpu32(n)
    4 * sum(curand(Float32, n).^2 .+ curand(Float32, n).^2 .<= 1) / n
end
```

As shown in the following code, we run this function on the GPU, expecting lower accuracy, but a significant speedup:

```
julia> @btime pi_gpu32(10_000_000)
  1.513 ms (158 allocations: 6.02 KiB)
3.1403428
```

As we would expect, using Float32 made the code run about twice as quickly. If your algorithm can work with the precision of 32 bits of floating point, it can be hugely advantageous to use that instead of Float64.

Writing your own kernels

The Julia CUDA packages allow the programmer to create their own low-level kernels for the GPU, where you write code to manually handle the parallelism. This is something unique in Julia—the ability to use a high-level language to write these kernels. Previously, CUDA C++ was pretty much the only option to implement your own kernel.

As an example, consider a simple function that adds two vectors in place. A kernel can be written as follows:

```
function add_gpu!(y, x)
    index = threadIdx().x
    stride = blockDim().x
        for i = index:stride:length(y)
          @inbounds y[i] += x[i]
        end
      return nothing
end
```

This is fairly low-level code, but is still recognizably Julia, while the semantics would be familiar to anyone who has written CUDA C. It parallelizes the code among the many threads, with every thread getting a reference to its own ID. This facilitates assigning unique work to each thread. This function can be run on an array with a million elements, running on 256 parallel threads as shown in the following code:

```
N=1000_000
a = cufill(1.0f0, N)
b = cufill(2.0f0, N)
@cuda threads=256 add_gpu!(b, a)
```

Using `CuArrays`, therefore, usually consists of creating arrays of numbers on the GPU, and then broadcasting kernels of computation over those arrays. While a detailed knowledge of CUDA programming is probably required for writing complex kernels in Julia, it is possible to use the built-in functionality to accelerate many algorithms using high-level dynamic code that is idiomatically Julia.

Measuring GPU performance

We've been using our trusty `@btime` macro from the `BenchmarkTools` package to measure the performance in this and previous chapters. While that works well, there are some GPU-specific methods that may occasionally be preferable.

First, the `CuArrays.@sync` macro may be used to force the execution of asynchronous kernels. These are usually only executed when its results are required by downstream processes, but that obviously invalidates the performance measurement. The `CuArrays.@sync` macro mitigates this issue by forcing the computation to occur within the timing loop. We show this using a trivial identity function. It is the difference between the two invocations as follows, which should be instructive:

```julia
julia> a = CuArray{Float32}(undef, 1024);

julia> @btime identity.($a);
  9.200 μs (51 allocations: 1.83 KiB)

julia> @btime CuArrays.@sync(identity.($a));
  38.199 μs (55 allocations: 1.94 KiB)
```

Note, however, that whenever you copy data back to the CPU, the code is forced to run, and `@sync` is not required when measuring. This copy can be implicit, for example, when displaying an output in the REPL. On the other hand, in these situations, you are also measuring the time to copy the data from the GPU to the CPU. So be cognizant of what exactly you are measuring.

Next, the `CuArrays.@time` macro provides estimates for the amount of memory allocation on the GPU. Like the `@time` macro, it runs the code only once, and hence cannot be statistically reliable as it can be affected by other programs running at the same time. However, using it to see the allocations is very useful, as shown here:

```julia
julia> CuArrays.@time pi_gpu(10_000_000)
  2.809474 seconds (3.86 M CPU allocations: 203.457 MiB, 3.47% gc time) (4
GPU allocations: 162.125 MiB, 0.16% gc time of which 97.08% spent
allocating)
3.1412844
```

Finally, the CUDA toolkit includes `nvprof`, which allows the profiling of code running on the GPU. It works perfectly well with Julia code and can be used to optimize kernels written in Julia.

Take a look at the following session output. We start the process by loading `nvprof` from the shell and asking it to load `julia`:

```
$ nvprof --profile-from-start off julia
```

Once Julia is loaded, we can use it normally to define our functions as follows:

```julia
julia> using CuArrays.CURAND
==81== NVPROF is profiling process 81, command: julia
```

```
julia> function pi_gpu(n)
           4 * sum(curand(Float64, n).^2 .+ curand(Float64, n).^2 .<= 1) / n
       end
pi_gpu (generic function with 1 method)
```

Now, we are ready to profile our GPU function. We run the code under the
`CUDAdrv.@profile` macro to collect and store the profile information, as follows:

```
julia> using CUDAdrv

julia> CUDAdrv.@profile begin
               pi_gpu(10_000_000)
           end;
```

Once our function is complete, we exit the Julia process, at which point `nvprof` will show
us the profiling results for our function like so:

```
julia>exit()
==81== Profiling application: julia
==81== Profiling result:
 Type Time(%) Time Calls Avg Min Max Name

GPU activities:
      51.17% 1.9049ms 2 952.44us 949.94us 954.94us void
 gen_sequenced<curandStateXORWOW, double,int, __operator_&__(double
 curand_uniform_double_noargs<curandStateXORWOW>(curandStateXORWOW*,
 int))>(curandStateXORWOW*, double*, unsigned long, unsigned long, int)

      34.62% 1.2889ms 1 1.2889ms 1.2889ms 1.2889ms ptxcall_anonymous23_1
      14.04% 522.52us 1 522.52us 522.52us 522.52us ptxcall_reduce_kernel_3
      0.09% 3.3600us 1 3.3600us 3.3600us 3.3600us ptxcall_anonymous19_2
      0.08% 2.8800us 1 2.8800us 2.8800us 2.8800us [CUDA memcpy DtoH]
API calls:
      72.35% 10.415ms 2 5.2076ms 21.800us 10.393ms cudaLaunch
      20.33% 2.9267ms 1 2.9267ms 2.9267ms 2.9267ms cuMemcpyDtoH
      6.89% 992.39us 4 248.10us 137.60us 404.80us cuMemAlloc
      0.35% 49.699us 3 16.566us 11.500us 20.000us cuLaunchKernel
      0.02% 3.5000us 4 875ns 200ns 2.0000us cudaGetLastError
      0.02% 2.8000us 1 2.8000us 2.8000us 2.8000us cuDeviceGetCount
      0.02% 2.2000us 9 244ns 200ns 300ns cuCtxGetCurrent
      0.01% 2.1000us 10 210ns 100ns 800ns cudaSetupArgument
      0.01% 1.2000us 2 600ns 400ns 800ns cudaConfigureCall
      0.00% 300ns 1 300ns 300ns 300ns cuCtxGetDevice
```

This profile tells us that we spend 72% of the time on launching the CUDA environment and 20% of time copying data from the device (GPU) to the host (CPU).

Performance tips

I hope you are convinced now that the GPU provides a massive boost to the performance of your code. However, the nature of a GPU constrains the design of your code significantly. The best-performing programs on the GPU will be those that are designed with these constraints in mind. These usually boil down to two specific criteria: copying data from CPU to GPU memory is slow, and a single GPU thread is also very slow. Thus, to take full advantage of the power of the GPU, ensure that data is not copied repeatedly to the GPU, and also ensure that your algorithm can be run fully parallel without any bottlenecks or choke points.

Scalar iteration

In all the code we have seen previously, we have used `broadcast` to apply a function over an array. This is the paradigm that provides the fastest GPU code. The converse, iterating on each element on an array one by one (scalar iteration), is prohibitively slow on the GPU.

As an example, say we want to add each column in a matrix to its neighbor on the right. Consider the following code that does this operation via scalar iteration:

```
function addcol_scalar(a, b)
    s = size(a)
    for j = 1:s[2]
        for i = 1:s[1]
            @inbounds a[i,j] = b[i,j+1] + b[i,j]
        end
    end
end
```

Next, we rewrite this function to add each column in one operation using broadcasting as follows:

```
function addcol_fast(a, b)
    s = size(a)
    for j = 1:s[2]
        @inbounds a[:,j] .= b[:,j+1] + b[:,j]
    end
end
```

To set a baseline, we create the dataset, and time the scalar code on the CPU, as shown here:

```
julia> a = ones(Float32, 10000, 99);

julia> b = ones(Float32, 10000, 100);

julia> @btime addcol_scalar($a, $b)
  338.195 μs (0 allocations: 0 bytes)
```

To execute these functions on the GPU, we copy the arrays to the GPU using the `CuArray` constructor. Note that the code does not change at all!

When timing these functions on the GPU, however, we see some terrible performance on the version that performs scalar iterations. It is so slow that we need to reduce the number of samples we use to measure performance, as shown in the following code:

```
julia> @btime addcol_scalar($(CuArray(a)), $(CuArray(b))) samples=2;
  30.473 s (14850000 allocations: 664.67 MiB)

julia> @btime addcol_fast($(CuArray(a)), $(CuArray(b)));
  5.027 ms (23265 allocations: 931.22 KiB)
```

This performance is so bad that we would usually not want to inadvertently hit these issues. If, by mistake, we write code in this manner, we would like to be warned. Hence, Julia provides the functionality to actually disable scalar iteration, so that any code that attempts to execute in this manner will throw an error, as shown in the following code:

```
julia> CuArrays.allowscalar(false)
false

julia> addcol_scalar(CuArray(a), CuArray(b))
ERROR: scalar getindex is disallowed
Stacktrace:
 [1] error(::String) at ./error.jl:33
 [2] assertscalar at
/home/jrun/.julia/packages/GPUArrays/t8tJB/src/indexing.jl:8 [inlined]
 [3] getindex(::CuArray{Float32,2}, ::Int64) at
/home/jrun/.julia/packages/GPUArrays/t8tJB/src/indexing.jl:44
 [4] _getindex at ./abstractarray.jl:928 [inlined]
 [5] getindex at ./abstractarray.jl:905 [inlined]
 [6] addcol_scalar(::CuArray{Float32,2}, ::CuArray{Float32,2}) at
./REPL[2]:5
 [7] top-level scope at none:0
```

This setting, therefore, provides a safety net for erroneous code; it will throw an error instead of executing the code thousands of times slower.

Combining kernels

In the optimized version of the code in the previous section, we used a broadcast to operate on each column of the array at a time. However, we still loop over the available columns. If we can remove that loop, then broadcast fusion can combine everything into one kernel. That would be much faster than the code we had earlier. Let's try that out. In the following code, we broadcast the addition over a two-dimensional slice, using the `@views` macro to prevent creating copies as we take slices:

```
function addcol_faster(a, b)
    a .= @views b[:, 2:end] .+ b[:, 1:end-1]
end
```

This code will now run much faster than what we had before—more than two orders of magnitude faster—and it is now faster than the CPU version:

```
julia> @btime addcol_faster($a, $b)
  325.996 µs (2 allocations: 128 bytes)

julia> @btime addcol_faster($(CuArray(a)), $(CuArray(b))) ;
  7.575 µs (39 allocations: 2.06 KiB)
```

To hit high performance on the GPU, therefore, we must try to use a single kernel over the entire dataset as far as possible.

Processing more data

Let's now try to run this code, both on the CPU and the GPU, with a hundred times more data, as shown in the following code:

```
julia> a = ones(Float32,1000_000, 99);

julia> b = ones(Float32, 1000_000, 100);

julia> @btime addcol_faster($a, $b);
  95.808 ms (2 allocations: 128 bytes)

julia> @btime addcol_faster($(CuArray(a)), $(CuArray(b))) ;
  7.925 µs (39 allocations: 2.06 KiB)
```

The timing results show that, as we increase the size of the data by a factor of 100, the time of execution on the CPU increases by almost a factor of 300, but the time on the GPU is near constant. So, to get the best out of a GPU, it is important to work on the large data sizes that can take full advantage of the parallelism available within it.

Deep learning on the GPU

The spread of deep learning methodologies has coincided with the popularity of the GPU in computing. These methods are very amenable to parallelization. Indeed, a lot of deep learning methods would not be feasible without GPUs.

Running deep learning models on the GPU requires the installation of the CuDNN library from NVIDIA. This library contains fast implementations of the low-level mathematical primitives needed for deep learning systems. You'll need to register with the NVIDIA Developer Network and then download the library from `https://developer.nvidia.com/cudnn`. Choose the version for your operating system and install it on your machine. You'll need to have installed the appropriate graphics drivers and the CUDA toolkit prior to installing CuDNN.

These primitives are now ready to be used from a higher-level library. To demonstrate, we use *Flux*, the pure Julia deep learning library. We will see how easy Flux makes it to use the GPU for training a deep learning model. Effectively, a single function is all it takes to move data and computations to the GPU.

 MNIST (or, Modified National Institute of Standards and Technology) is a standardized dataset of handwritten numbers that can be used to train handwriting recognition models. It is widely used in machine learning to test the efficiency and accuracy of ML techniques. It's useful as a well-defined problem with cleaned, labeled data.

To begin, here is the code to train a convolution neural network using the **MNIST** dataset:

1. First, we import the packages as follows:

```
using Flux, Flux.Data.MNIST, Statistics
using Flux: onehotbatch, onecold, crossentropy, throttle
using Base.Iterators: repeated, partition
```

2. Then, load the image data into memory, as shown here:

```
imgs = MNIST.images();
```

3. We encode the label (in other words, the number being recognized) in *one-hot* form as follows:

```
labels = onehotbatch(MNIST.labels(), 0:9)
```

4. As shown in the following code, we also split the data into training and test sets, and partition the training data into batches for training:

```
## Partition into batches of size 32
train = [(cat(float.(imgs[i])..., dims = 4), labels[:,i])
    for i in partition(1:60_000, 32)]
## Prepare test set (first 1,000 images)
tX = cat(float.(MNIST.images(:test)[1:1000])..., dims = 4)
tY = onehotbatch(MNIST.labels(:test)[1:1000], 0:9)
```

5. Once the data is loaded, we create a neural network model that we expect to be able to recognize the handwritten digits. This neural network consists of a series of layers, some of which are convolutions, along with a final dense layer. This is shown in the following code:

```
m = Chain(
  Conv((3, 3), 1=>32, relu),
  Conv((3, 3), 32=>32, relu),
  x -> maxpool(x, (2,2)),
  Conv((3, 3), 32=>16, relu),
  x -> maxpool(x, (2,2)),
  Conv((3, 3), 16=>10, relu),
  x -> reshape(x, :, size(x, 4)),
  Dense(90, 10), softmax)
```

6. To train the model, we define a `loss` function that we need to optimize and the optimizer that we use for this purpose. In this case, we choose to use the ADAM optimizer. We also define a function to calculate the accuracy of our model, which is based on the difference between the predicted and actual labels:

```
loss(x, y) = crossentropy(m(x), y)
accuracy(x, y) = mean(onecold(m(x)) .== onecold(y))
opt = ADAM()
```

7. Now, running this on the GPU is simply a matter of using the `gpu` function to move the data into the GPU, as shown here:

```
gputrain = gpu.(train)
gpum = gpu(m)
gputX = gpu(tX)
gputY = gpu(tY)
gpuloss(x, y) = crossentropy(gpum(x), y)
gpuaccuracy(x, y) = mean(onecold(gpum(x) |> cpu) .== onecold(y) |>
cpu)
```

8. Note that both the model itself and all the input data (the features and labels) need to be moved to the GPU. Once that is done, your deep learning model is training on the GPU without any other change to your code, and running many times faster, as evidenced in the following code:

```
julia> @time Flux.train!(loss, Flux.params(m), train, opt)
151.189526 seconds (40.03 M allocations: 56.163 GiB, 4.13% gc time)

julia> @time Flux.train!(gpuloss, Flux.params(gpum), gputrain, opt)
14.439104 seconds (15.45 M allocations: 1012.658 MiB, 2.30% gc
time)
```

9. The actual speedup will depend on the nature of your GPU and your model, but an improvement of many orders of magnitude is possible.

   With the model trained, we can now measure its accuracy on the test data we kept behind like so:

```
julia> @show accuracy(tX, tY);
accuracy(tX, tY) = 0.972

julia> @show gpuaccuracy(gputX, gputY);
gpuaccuracy(gputX, gputY) = 0.972
```

We can verify that the two models have similar accuracy. The speed of training on the GPU is not achieved at the cost of the quality of the model.

ArrayFire

The ArrayFire library provides a high-level abstraction that makes writing massively parallel programs much simpler to write. The underlying library is written in C++, and the Julia wrapper provides an Array abstraction that allows idiomatic Julia programs to be executed on the GPU.

To begin, install the ArrayFire library for your operating system from https://arrayfire.com/download/ and install it on your GPU machine. Once installed, ArrayFire provides a wrapper around an array that copies data from the CPU to the GPU, and performs operations on that data on the GPU cores. It really is that simple.

In the following example, we create a random 2D matrix, copy it to the GPU, multiply it by itself, and then copy the result back to the main memory:

```
julia> using ArrayFire

julia> a=rand(1000,1000);
1000×1000 Array{Float64,2}:
...

julia> b=AFArray(a)
AFArray: 1000×1000 Array{Float64,2}:
...

julia> c=b*b;

julia> d=Array(c)
```

Timing the operations, we see significant speedups in terms of operating on the GPU. We first measure the time taken to multiply a matrix with itself as follows:

```
julia> @btime $b*$b;
  4.848 ms (1 allocation: 16 bytes)

julia> @btime $a*$a;
  10.425 ms (2 allocations: 7.63 MiB)
```

Even more significant speedups can be seen in transcendental functions element-wise on the matrix, as shown here:

```
julia> @btime begin; sin($b); sync($b); end;
  3.237 μs (1 allocation: 16 bytes)

julia> @btime sin.($a);
  9.012 ms (2 allocations: 7.63 MiB)
```

This invocation shows the real power of the GPU. Unlike a matrix multiplication, in this case, the computation can be parallelized over all one million elements of the array. Also, note that many `ArrayFire` operations are asynchronous—they are executed only when their results are required by downstream operations. This makes benchmarking more complicated, hence, the `sync` functions that force the operations to execute. There is usually no need to do that when writing real-world programs with `ArrayFire`.

Note that when we benchmark these operations, we have not measured the cost of copying the data from the CPU memory to the GPU memory and back. In a practical algorithm, this overhead will matter, so it's important to think about how and when that occurs. The best case scenario, as before, is when data is transferred to the GPU once, and then many expensive operations are executed on that data. The alternative, where data is transferred multiple times from the CPU to GPU, or vice versa, is terrible in this context—where the overhead of data transfer will kill any performance improvement from the GPU.

Summary

This chapter provided an introduction to using Julia code on the GPU. It showed you how to install the relevant libraries and compile Julia to the GPU. Copying data to the GPU and processing it there is one of the most efficient ways to accelerate your code. If your code is amenable to high parallelization and can fit within the GPU's memory, then nothing comes close in terms of making your code fast. The whole deep learning revolution is proof of its success.

In the next chapter, we will go back to the CPU, and see how the tasks and asynchronous I/O can help accelerate your code.

8
Concurrent Programming with Tasks

Most programs in Julia run on a single thread, on a single processor core. In other words, most processing in Julia is synchronous. But we know that a modern computer can appear to do many things in parallel. It can play music while you are writing a report, run your tests when you are typing code, or run a web server in the background. There are many layers to achieving this level of multiprocessing. In this chapter, we will look at concurrent primitives that make it possible to run parallel, or seemingly parallel operations, without the full complexities of shared memory multithreading. We will discuss how the concept of co-operative multitasking, implemented as tasks and asynchronous I/O, helps create responsive programs. The following are the topics we will cover in this chapter:

- Tasks
- Controlling tasks with the @sync and @async macros
- Using channels to communicate between tasks
- High-performance **input/output (I/O)**

Tasks

A Task is simply a set of instructions that can be suspended and resumed at any point within that set. A function could also be thought of as a set of instructions, and hence tasks can be seen as something similar. But there are two crucial differences—one, there is no overhead to switching between one task to another, meaning, no stack space is reserved for a switch. Second, unlike a function that has to finish before control goes back to the caller, a task can be interrupted and control switched to another at many different times during its execution. In other words, there is no caller-callee hierarchical relationship in tasks.

Tasks can provide the illusion of having two parallel sequences of instructions running simultaneously on the computer. It is important to note that with tasks, only one of those sequences is running on the CPU at any one point. Tasks do not typically take advantage of multiple CPU cores on a machine. However, by switching between those sequences, the illusion that they are running simultaneously can be maintained.

There is one other crucial factor to consider. We said that a task can be interrupted to run another. But this can only happen at specified points during execution when the code explicitly signals that it is ready to hand back control to another. A supervisory scheduler cannot interrupt a task at any arbitrary point in time.

A task can signal that it is ready to be interrupted using the `yield` function. This returns control back to the scheduler, which can then run another task at that point. But more likely, any I/O activity done in a task creates an opportunity for that task to yield, since Julia uses asynchronous I/O using the Libuv library. **Libuv** is a C library that provides capabilities for many low-level operations on a machine in an OS agnostic manner. Since it was built to be used with Node.js, it's designed to be used in a highly asynchronous manner. This allows Julia to use separate tasks for all I/O, and thus, creates opportunities for pervasive asynchronous task usage within Julia programs.

Using tasks

Consider the following trivial code. How long do you think this will take?

```
for i in 1:5
    sleep(1)
end
```

Well, the answer is obviously five seconds—a sleep of one second at a time, executed five times, as shown in the following code:

```
julia> @time for i in 1:5
           sleep(1)
       end
  5.026456 seconds (26 allocations: 1.266 KiB)
```

Now see what happens when we write this code with the `@async` macro, as follows:

```
julia> @time for i in 1:5
           @async sleep(1)
       end
  0.000140 seconds (32 allocations: 4.375 KiB)
```

The @async macro (short for *asynchronous*) creates and schedules tasks for all code within its scope (in this case, the sleep(1) function call), which means all the sleep calls happen in separate tasks. The for loop, which is running on the REPL task, returns almost immediately. Since the for loop returns, we cannot even observe the sleep occurring. It happens completely in the background.

If we want the for loop to wait and observe the execution of the tasks started within it, we use the @sync macro. As shown in the following code, the @sync macro will pause a task until all tasks created by it have finished execution:

```julia
julia> @time @sync for i in 1:5
           @async sleep(1)
       end
  1.023581 seconds (1.86 k allocations: 91.036 KiB)
```

As before, the @async macro inside the for loop creates five tasks. Those tasks contain the sleep function call, which enables it to yield; this allows all the tasks to start nearly simultaneously. Further, the sleep function itself does not take CPU resources. As a result, all the tasks also finish at almost the same time. This time, however, the for loop does not return and waits for the sleep function to complete. As a result, the whole operation takes approximately one second. Put another way, five sleeps of one second each run sequentially takes five seconds, but the same five sleeps run in parallel takes one second.

As we said in the previous section, the parallelism is somewhat simulated. While tasks can be interrupted and switch between one another, at any one time, only one task is running on the CPU. Thus, you will see a performance benefit only for code that is doing something but not taking CPU resources—this typically means it is waiting for some I/O, or as in the degenerate case previously, sleeping. Hence this pattern of code is useful in programs that are I/O heavy—where code spends a lot of time waiting for disk or network data.

If we try this pattern on code that is CPU-intensive, then we will see no improvement. For one, there is no opportunity in this code for the task to yield. And even if it could, every task will fully utilize the CPU, thereby showing no improvement in the elapsed time.

The following code demonstrates this fact, showing very little improvement in running the `sin` function for multiple tasks:

```julia
julia> @time for i in 1:50
           sin.(rand(1000, 1000))
       end
 1.404643 seconds (200 allocations: 762.947 MiB, 18.04% gc time)


julia> @time @sync for i in 1:50
           @async sin.(rand(1000, 1000))
       end
 1.132099 seconds (28.27 k allocations: 764.256 MiB, 11.31% gc time)
```

In addition, tasks can be interrupted only when they allow themselves to be. In other words, tasks have to yield in order for other tasks to run. Operations that include I/O and sleep yield implicitly when waiting for events. Other tasks have to yield explicitly via the `yield` function. A particular consideration in this context is the fact that, once you call into a C function from Julia, the scheduler can no longer interrupt that code. Even if I/O or sleep occurs on the C side, from Julia's perspective, it is a blocking call, and no task switching can occur before the C function call returns.

The following is written in the same way as the code shown previously, but instead of using Julia's built-in sleep function, which yields, we call into the C standard library to run its `sleep` function. In this case, the task does not yield, and we get serial performance even if we create separate tasks with `@async`:

```julia
julia> @time @sync for i in 1:5
           @async ccall(("sleep", :libc), Cint, (Cint, ), 1)
       end
 5.074224 seconds (61.10 k allocations: 2.931 MiB)
```

This code takes five seconds, showing that the tasks are run consecutively, not in parallel.

The task life cycle

While tasks are easily created using the `@async` macro, they can also be created directly. They are represented by the `Task` object, whose constructor typically takes a function that needs to execute in the context of the task. This needs to be a zero-argument function, as follows:

```julia
julia> t=Task(()->println("Hello from tasks"))
Task (runnable) @0x0000000110ff58d0
```

The state of a task can be queried by the `istaskdone` and `istaskstarted` function, as follows:

```
julia> istaskstarted(t)
false

julia> istaskdone(t)
false
```

Once created, the task can then be passed to Julia's scheduler, which will queue up all tasks, and switch to them when appropriate. In this case, since we are on the REPL (which yields often), that task begins as soon as it is scheduled. And once scheduled, we see that the status of the `Task` changes as well.

We illustrate this in the following code snippet:

```
julia> schedule(t)
Hello from tasks
Task (queued) @0x0000000110e98b50

julia> istaskdone(t)
true

julia> istaskstarted(t)
true
```

The `current_task` function returns the currently running task as follows:

```
julia> current_task()
Task (runnable) @0x000000010f6786d0

julia> t == current_task()
false
```

While not very useful for user code, the `current_task` function is crucial for the implementation of `task_local_storage`, which we discuss in the next section.

task_local_storage

The `task_local_storage` function allows each task to keep data of its own, scoped by the life cycle of the task itself. This allows multiple functions running within a task to communicate and store data, without using a global value. The values stored in `task_local_storage` is isolated within that task as follows:

```julia
julia> task_local_storage("x", 1)
1

julia> task_local_storage("x") == 1
true
```

One example of using this could be within a web server, where each request is handled by a separate task, and some request parameters could be stored in `task_local_storage`.

Communicating between tasks

When multiple tasks are running simultaneously, it is useful sometimes to be able to communicate data and state between them. A `Channel` is a Julia object that can be used to asynchronously send data from one task to another. A `Channel` is created by specifying the type of object it can contain, and a maximum number of elements it can hold. If no type is specified, `Any` is used. A maximum value of `0` implies that the channel can hold an unlimited number of values.

The following code snippet shows how to create a channel:

```julia
julia> c = Channel{Int}(10)
Channel{Int64}(sz_max:10,sz_curr:0)
```

A channel should be viewed as a pipe, with data entering at one end, and being consumed at the other. Values are sent to the channel using the `put!` function, and taken using the `take!` function. The `put!` function will block if the channel is at capacity, while the `take!` function is blocked if the channel is empty. Typically, the filling and emptying of the channel is done by different tasks, which allows them to communicate with each other in an asynchronous fashion.

One useful example is in using this to create a producer-consumer pattern. This entails creating values in one task and using them in another. The first task can thus send data to another task asynchronously.

We start by defining a function that fills values into a provided channel as follows:

```
function producer(c::Channel)
    put!(c, "start")
    for n=1:4
        put!(c, 2n)
    end
    put!(c, "stop")
end
```

We then create a `Channel`. The constructor `Channel` takes another function as an argument. This latter function fills the `Channel` using a task. Subsequently, we can extract the values from the `Channel` as required:

```
julia> chnl = Channel(producer)
Channel{Any}(sz_max:0,sz_curr:1)

julia> take!(chnl)
 "start"

julia> take!(chnl)
 2

julia> take!(chnl)
 4

julia> take!(chnl)
 6

julia> take!(chnl)
 8

julia> take!(chnl)
 "stop"
```

It is important to note that the filling of values in the channel occurs in a task that is different from the consuming of values. The filling happens in the new task created by the `Channel` constructor, while the consumption happens in the REPL task. This asynchronous data transfer is a key aspect of using Channels and Tasks effectively.

Task iteration

A crucial feature of Channels is that they are iterators. In other words, you can write a `for` loop over a channel. This allows for elegant code when working with `Tasks` and `Channels`.

Continuing with the producer-consumer example used previously, the values can be consumed via a `for` loop as follows:

```julia
julia> chnl = Channel(producer)
Channel{Any}(sz_max:0,sz_curr:1)

julia> for i in chnl
           @show i
       end
i = "start"
i = 2
i = 4
i = 6
i = 8
i = "stop"
```

The loop continues until the channel is closed. In this case, the channel we created is closed implicitly when the task is complete, which in turn happens when the `producer` function returns. When needed, however, the `close(chnl)` function can be used to explicitly close a channel.

The following code shows the asynchronous iteration performed on a channel. I would suggest you run this code interactively, one step at a time, to fully understand the behavior:

```julia
julia> function consume(c)
           println("Starting Channel iteration")
           for i in c
               println("Got $i from Channel")
           end
           println("Channel iteration is complete")
       end
consume (generic function with 1 method)

julia> chnl = Channel(1)
Channel{Any}(sz_max:1,sz_curr:0)

julia> @async consume(chnl)
Starting Channel iteration
Task (queued) @0x0000000110e98910

julia> put!(chnl, 1)
Got 1 from Channel
1

julia> put!(chnl, 2)
Got 2 from Channel
2

julia> close(chnl)
Channel iteration is complete
```

Running this code, you will notice that not only will you get each value from the channel asynchronously, but also, the consume loop will keep going until you close the channel explicitly.

High-performance I/O

All I/O in Julia is built on top of libuv, an abstraction library originally built for use with Node.js. As we said earlier, this allows Julia to use a high-quality, OS-independent library for all I/O. Reading and writing to and from disks, networks, and terminals are all handled within it.

As a library built for Node.js, it is not a surprise that the libuv API is built around asynchronous I/O. However, Julia's task system makes it much easier to use from Julia. You do not have to write callback functions to handle return values from I/O calls. The code you write appears to be synchronous, straight-line code. Under the hood, the calls are made in a non-blocking manner. Not only is the current task yielded to allow other Julia code to run; all I/O is multiplexed onto a separate operating system thread, thereby allowing multiple I/O tasks to operate seemingly simultaneously, as we saw earlier in this chapter.

Port sharing for high-performance web serving

Julia can, of course, be used for many use cases beyond scientific computing. Writing a web server is one such common requirement. A web server typically needs to serve requests from multiple users simultaneously. Moreover, by its very nature, a web server is a network I/O-intensive application. As a result, using separate tasks to process each request is easy to do within a Julia web server.

This model is, however, limited to running the process on one CPU core. Further, if part of the request processing pipeline involves calling into C code (say, in a database driver), that will block the main Julia process, and hence, all requests on the server. When scaling up a web server, however, to a large machine, it is useful to consider running the process on all cores. In Julia, this will necessitate running multiple Julia processes, the details of which we will see in Chapter 10, *Distributed Computing with Julia*.

Running a web server on multiple processes, however, causes a problem. We want clients to send requests to a single port, but usually, that port is bound to a single process by the operating system. Typically, running web servers on multiple processes on a single server needs some kind of a proxy system to be set up.

Julia, however, supports the concept of port sharing, where multiple processes can share the same listening port. The OS will typically mediate the requests, and send them to each process in a round-robin fashion. Using the Julia web framework, `Mux` (which can be installed via the package manager), we see this in action with the `resuseaddr` argument, as shown in the following code:

```
using Mux
@app basicapp = (
        Mux.defaults,
        page("/", respond("<h1>Hello World!</h1>")),
        Mux.notfound())

serve(basicapp; reuseaddr=true)
```

With this invocation, this code will run successfully on multiple Julia processes, all of whom will now respond to client requests on the same port. Similar code can be written using the `HTTP.jl` package as well. That package provides the underlying web server implementation that `Mux` uses.

Summary

In this chapter, we saw how Julia supports asynchronous programming using `Tasks`. Co-operative multiprocessing allows programs to do more than one thing at a time, while still using a single CPU and following a simple memory usage model. In the next chapter, we will explore shared memory multiprocessing using threads, where different CPU cores might be running Julia code simultaneously in parallel.

9
Threads

In the last chapter, we saw how tasks provide a simple way to run multiple streams of compute, even on a single CPU core, when there is I/O involved. However, as the modern CPU has grown to include multiple cores that all operate simultaneously, we need to be able to execute Julia code on them in parallel. The way to do that is typically described as threads or threading, and, in this chapter, we will talk about the facilities Julia provides to run programs on multiple CPU cores simultaneously.

We will begin by noting that Julia's threading features are marked *experimental*. They are still useful, as you will see in this chapter. However, there is a large internal refactoring that is currently underway. It is expected that these will land in Julia versions 1.3 onward. These changes will make these features more robust, and high-performance, and remove some of their current limitations.

There are two main limitations associated with the current threading primitives that I should warn you about. The first is that most I/Os in Julia's standard library are not thread-safe—you should not perform I/O operations in multithreaded code. The other is that nested threading is not supported very well. However, as you continue your journey as a Julia developer, be on the lookout for these to be fixed in future versions.

So, in this chapter, we will show you how to write multithreaded Julia programs in ways that guarantee both safety and high performance. Topics we'll discuss include the following:

- Threads, their life cycle, and the `@threads` macro
- Thread safety and synchronization primitives
- Threads and libraries

Threads

Threads are sequences of computation that can run independently on a CPU core, simultaneously with other such sequences. So, one of the first questions we need to ask ourselves is: how many threads should we have? Unlike tasks, which are lightweight, threads need to store some state when they are switched. Thus, while you can have hundreds or thousands of tasks in your program, you should only have a limited number of threads. The general advice is that the number of threads should correspond directly to the number of CPU cores you have.

Measuring CPU cores

So, how many CPU cores do you have? The answer might not be so easy to get to. One particular complication is hyper-threading. This is a facility that Intel CPUs have that allows a single core to seemingly run multiple streams of compute in parallel. However, this parallelism is again simulated, and only one CPU instruction is actually executed at one time. For CPU intensive programs, hyper-threading usually does not provide much benefit. So what we really want to count are physical CPU cores—independent pieces of silicon.

This issue is apparent if you do use the verbose mode of the `versioninfo` function in Julia to view system information.

The following output shows you the hyper-threading cores, since the operating system will count hyper-threading cores independently. With two hyper-threading cores per physical core, this will typically show you double the number of cores you have:

```
julia> versioninfo(verbose=true)
Julia Version 1.1.0
Commit 80516ca202 (2019-01-21 21:24 UTC)
Platform Info:
  OS: macOS (x86_64-apple-darwin14.5.0)
  uname: Darwin 18.2.0 Darwin Kernel Version 18.2.0: Mon Nov 12 20:24:46 PST
2018; root:xnu-4903.231.4~2/RELEASE_X86_64 x86_64 i386
  CPU: Intel(R) Core(TM) i5-4258U CPU @ 2.40GHz:
      speed user nice sys idle irq
    #1 2400 MHz 2015893 s 0 s 1287368 s 10784841 s 0 s
    #2 2400 MHz 1110726 s 0 s 557999 s 12418983 s 0 s
    #3 2400 MHz 2020641 s 0 s 1031956 s 11035112 s 0 s
    #4 2400 MHz 1044809 s 0 s 442534 s 12600366 s 0 s

Memory: 8.0 GB (43.94140625 MB free)
  Uptime: 3.856531e6 sec
  Load Avg: 2.05078125 1.85888671875 1.857421875
  WORD_SIZE: 64
  LIBM: libopenlibm
  LLVM: libLLVM-6.0.1 (ORCJIT, haswell)
```

On macOS, in recent versions of the operating system, the number of physical CPU cores can be seen using the *System Information* application. Click on the **Apple menu**, then **About this Mac**, and finally, on **System Report**. That will show you, among other things, detailed information about your CPU as follows:

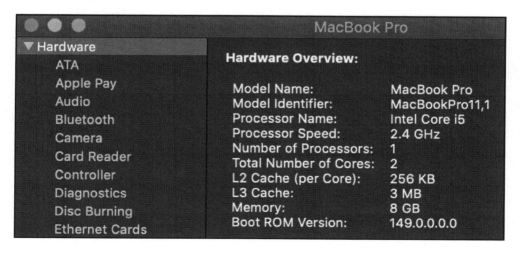

On computers running Windows 10, the number of physical cores can be viewed in the **Task Manager** application. Start the **Task Manager** by pressing *Ctrl + Shift + Esc*, and then click on the **Performance** tab, as shown in the following screenshot:

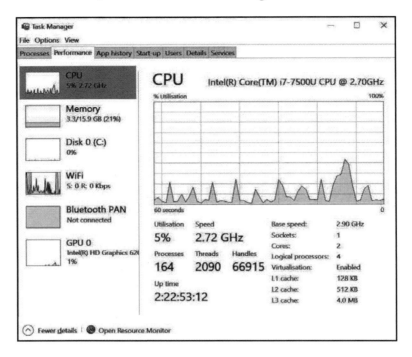

On Linux, `cat /proc/cpuinfo` will list each hyper-threaded processor separately, but part of the listing will also show you the number of physical cores on the system

Hwloc

As you can see, finding this information can be complex and is certainly system dependent. The `hwloc` library helps to provide uniform and programmatic information to this and other hardware information in a platform-agnostic fashion. To use this library, first install it using Julia's package manager as follows:

```
julia> using Pkg

julia> Pkg.add("Hwloc")
```

Once installed, this package provides many functions to probe the actual hardware you have. One such function is `num_physical_cores`, which, as you can see in the following code, will return the number of physical cores:

```
julia> using Hwloc

julia> Hwloc.num_physical_cores()
2
```

This package finally provides us with a consistent and correct enumeration of the number of physical CPU cores on the machine.

Starting threads

The number of real threads that Julia can run is fixed at startup. It depends on the `JULIA_NUM_THREADS` environmental variable and is checked when the Julia runtime starts up. If the variable is not set, the default number of threads is `1`:

```
$ export JULIA_NUM_THREADS = 4
```

Once Julia is started, you can check the number of threads using the `nthreads` function. This and other threading functionalities are located in the `Base.Threads` module, which we need to import into the following listing:

```
julia> using Base.Threads

julia> nthreads()
4
```

The `threadid` function returns the current thread ID as follows:

```
julia> threadid()
1
```

So, by default, all Julia code is running on the first thread. We can see this in the following code, where the first element of the array gets filled with the number 1 many times inside the loop:

```
julia> a=zeros(4)
4-element Array{Float64,1}:
 0.0
 0.0
 0.0
 0.0

julia> for i in 1:nthreads()
    a[threadid()] = threadid()
end

julia> a
4-element Array{Float64,1}:
 1.0
 0.0
 0.0
 0.0
```

Let's have a look at the @threads macro in the next section.

The @threads macro

In the for loop in the previous section, what we want is for each iteration of the loop to be executed on a different thread. Since the loop length is the same as the number of threads, we should see each iteration of the loop body run in a different thread. In Julia, that is very easy to achieve using the @threads macro, whose use is illustrated in the following code:

```
julia> @threads for i in 1:nthreads()
        a[threadid()] = threadid()
    end

julia> a
4-element Array{Float64,1}:
 1.0
 2.0
 3.0
 4.0
```

The array a is now filled in a way that proves each iteration of the loop ran on a separate thread, with different thread IDs.

This example code shows how simple Julia's threading model is, at least in how it is presented to the developer—the idea being that annotated loops are automatically split among available threads, without the programmer having to explicitly break up computations, or assign the code to threads. Of course, this involves a lot of effort in the compiler and runtime, but the facilities exposed to the Julia programmer are relatively simple.

Prefix sum

An interesting algorithm that is amenable to parallelization is prefix summation, also known as cumulative sum, or cumsum. Given an array, prefix sum returns another array; each element of the result is the sum of all elements in the input to the current index. Thus, the first element of the result is the same as the first element of the input. The second element of the result is the sum of the first and second elements of the input. The third element of the result is the sum of the first three elements of the input, and so on.

Here is a parallelized version of an optimized prefix sum, using the @threads macro:

```
function prefix_threads!(y)
    l=length(y)
    k=ceil(Int, log2(l))
    for j=1:k
        @threads for i=2^j:2^j:min(l, 2^k)
            @inbounds y[i] = y[i-2^(j-1)] + y[i]
        end
    end
    for j=(k-1):-1:1
        @threads for i=3*2^(j-1):2^j:min(l, 2^k)
            @inbounds y[i] = y[i-2^(j-1)] + y[i]
        end
    end
    y
end
```

 Details about the algorithm, and how Julia helps in expressing this, can be found in a paper by Jiahao Chen and Alan Edelman, *Parallel Prefix Polymorphism Permits Parallelization, Presentation & Proof*, available from https://arxiv.org/abs/1410.6449.

Thread safety and synchronization primitives

Threads imply code running simultaneously on multiple processor cores in a computer. The processors and the code running within them have access to the entire memory of the computer. This means that code in two threads can attempt to change the same piece of data in memory at the same time. As you can imagine, that would not be a good idea, and many different strategies have been created over the years to deal with this situation in multithreaded code.

Multithreaded Monte Carlo simulation

Remember the code we saw in `Chapter 7`, *Accelerating Code with the GPU*, to calculate the value of `pi` using *Monte Carlo simulation*. It used a loop to calculate a position based on draws from a random number generator. It should, therefore, be easy to run this in parallel across many threads.

Let's remind ourselves of the serial code:

```
using Random
function darts_in_circle(n, rng=Random.GLOBAL_RNG)
    inside = 0
    for i in 1:n
        if rand(rng)^2 + rand(rng)^2 < 1
            inside += 1
        end
    end
 return inside
end

function pi_serial(n)
    return 4 * darts_in_circle(n) / n
end
```

The simplest way to parallelize this function would be to add a `@threads` annotation in front of the `for` loop. However, that would be very wrong. Notice that the `rand()` function is called inside the `for` loop. This function generates a random number using a global random number generator, which is stateful. In other words, it changes its internal state every time a new number is generated; this means that when multiple threads try to generate random numbers simultaneously, we get the problem of multiple threads trying to change the same location in memory.

The fix, in this case, is relatively simple. We need to give each thread its own random number generator so that there is no contention for the data managed by separate threads. The following code sets up an array of independent random number generators, which we will then use in our threaded loop as follows:

```
julia> using Base.Threads

julia> const rnglist = [MersenneTwister() for i in 1:nthreads()]
```

Once the list of **Random Number Generators (RNGs)** has been set up, we write our loop to ensure that each thread uses a separate RNG. We achieve this once again by using the thread ID to index into the RNG list, as shown in the following code:

```
function pi_threads(n, loops)
    inside = zeros(Int, loops)
    @threads for i in 1:loops
        rng = rnglist[threadid()]
        inside[threadid()] = darts_in_circle(n, rng)
    end
    return 4 * sum(inside) / (n*loops)
end
```

There are a few things to notice in this code. One, we split up our problem into separate blocks for each thread. We do this explicitly, taking as input the number of threads, calling the function like so:

```
julia> pi_threads(2_500_000, 4)
3.141098
```

However, it could very well be done automatically based on the number of available threads. Our threaded loop must run over the total number of threads we have available. Inside each thread, we loop over a section of the entire problem, and, in the end, add the result to a per-thread element in the `inside` array.

As shown in the following code, timing the two functions, we see a two-fold improvement in performance, which is what we should expect on a machine with two CPU cores:

```
julia> @btime pi_serial(10_000_000)
  36.546 ms (0 allocations: 0 bytes)
3.1420988

julia> @btime pi_threads(2_500_000, 4)
  18.946 ms (2 allocations: 160 bytes)
3.1426036
```

In summary, in order to ensure performance gains in threaded code, it is important to ensure that each thread runs independently, with no global state.

> We created an independent random number generator for each thread. This may not be statistically accurate for pseudo-random number generators. It may be better to use `randjump` to ensure that each random number generator samples from a separate space. This function was recently introduced and lives in the `Future` module.

Atomics

We've shown many ways to sum numbers over the course of this book. Let's now try to sum an array of numbers across many threads, hoping to improve performance compared to doing it sequentially on a single thread.

Our first attempt, in the following code, simply tries to run the loop on multiple threads:

```
function sum_thread_base(x)
    r = zero(eltype(x))
    @threads for i in eachindex(x)
        @inbounds r += x[i]
    end
    return r
end
```

We can then compare this function against Julia's built-in sum as follows:

```
julia> a=rand(10_000_000);

julia> @btime sum($a)
  6.746 ms (0 allocations: 0 bytes)
5.000462435093071e6

julia> @btime sum_thread_base($a)
  1.566 s (5506561 allocations: 84.01 MiB)
1.250442324066673e6
```

The results may be surprising at first glance. Not only is the function producing the wrong answer, but it is also much slower. The problem with correctness may be apparent; inside the loop, we are trying to read and write to `r`, the result variable. Doing that simultaneously in multiple threads leads to wrong values, since one thread may be reading one value, and then trying to increment that, while another thread writes a different value before the first thread has finished.

One solution to this is to create r as an atomic variable. In this case, adding a value to r will be a single indivisible operation. That is, the act of adding a value to r (and writing the result back to r) will be an operation that cannot be interrupted by any other thread. The atomic addition is performed by the `atomic_add!` method, which works with an atomic variable. Using this facility in the following code fixes the error in the answer:

```
function sum_thread_atomic(x)
    r = Atomic{eltype(x)}(zero(eltype(x)))
    @threads for i in eachindex(x)
        @inbounds atomic_add!(r, x[i])
    end
    return r[]
end

julia> @btime sum_thread_atomic($a)
  883.710 ms (2 allocations: 48 bytes)
5.000462435092813e6
```

So, using an atomic add fixes our correctness issue. But the threaded addition is still much slower than sequential code. There are a couple of reasons for that. One, atomic operations are generally slower than regular operations. Furthermore, the use of atomic operations implies that only one thread (one CPU) can increment the sum at a time. As a result, the overall operation is significantly slower.

To make this faster, we will need to reduce the contention between threads. The following code demonstrates a way to break the sum so that different accumulators are used for different threads:

```
function sum_thread_split(A)
    r = Atomic{eltype(A)}(zero(eltype(A)))
    len, rem = divrem(length(A), nthreads())
    #Split the array equally among the threads
    @threads for t in 1:nthreads()
        r[] = zero(eltype(A))
        @simd for i in (1:len) .+ (t-1)*len
            @inbounds r[] += A[i]
        end
        atomic_add!(r, r[])
     end
    result = r[]
    #process up the remaining data
    @simd for i in length(A)-rem+1:length(A)
        @inbounds result += A[i]
    end
    return result
 end
```

This is more complicated than the simple code we started with, but that is the cost of using shared memory multithreading. Unlike the `pi_threads` function previously, we automatically split the data among available threads, without asking the programmer to provide this information. However, all of this does give us significant performance gains, which we can see when we benchmark the code as follows:

```
julia> @btime sum_thread_split($a)
  1.501 ms (2 allocations: 64 bytes)
5.000462435093066e6
```

And, even more importantly, it scales with increasing cores (and threads). When I run this code on a large 8-core machine with eight threads (`JULIA_NUM_THREADS=8`), I see further performance gains as shown here:

```
julia> @btime sum_thread_split($a)
   817.722 µs (2 allocations: 64 bytes)
```

There are many other atomic operations defined in Julia, beyond the `atomic_add!` function we saw. These operate in a similar fashion, ensuring that the operations happen in a thread-safe manner. These include `atomic_sub!`, `atomic_cas!`, `atomic_xchg!`, `atomic_and!`, and `atomic_or!`, among others. Full details are available at the Julia documentation site: `https://docs.julialang.org/en/v1/base/multi-threading/`.

Synchronization primitives

While the `@threads` macro (along with the atomic operations) provides a reasonably high-level abstraction for programming multithreaded applications, occasionally, you may need to use lower-level tools to coordinate and synchronize threaded code. Julia provides a traditional set of synchronization primitives, such as locks and semaphores. These primitives may be used to manage synchronization for both threads and tasks.

Locks, or mutexes, are used to guard resources and critical sections of code so that only one thread can access a resource at one time. As an example, say we want to run the `pi_serial` function we saw earlier to calculate the value of pi using Monte Carlo simulation. We want to run the simulation independently in many threads, and write the output from each thread into a file for later analysis.

While running the simulation in multiple threads is easy, since every run is independent, writing the output to file from each thread is not trivial. Multiple threads writing to the same file simultaneously is likely to corrupt that file. We can, however, protect access to the file using a mutex.

First, we create an output file to append, and define a mutex as follows:

```
julia> const f = open(tempname(), "a+")
IOStream(<file /tmp/juliaSfXHrs>)

julia> const m = Base.Threads.Mutex();
```

Next, we write a threaded loop, as shown in the following code, in which file access is protected by the mutex defined previously:

```
julia> @threads for i in 1:50
          r = pi_serial(10_000_000)
          lock(m)
          write(f, "From $(threadid()), pi = $r\n")
          unlock(m)
       end
```

The `lock` function acquires a lock (and blocks if the lock is not available), while the `unlock` function releases it. Each `lock` must be followed by an `unlock` from the same thread that acquired the lock.

We can inspect the file created to see that it has been successfully and cleanly written by multiple threads as follows:

```
julia> close(f)

shell> cat /tmp/juliaSfXHrs
From 4, pi = 3.1412404
From 2, pi = 3.1420044
From 6, pi = 3.1423572
From 1, pi = 3.1418848
```

There are other lock types available, such as the `Spinlock` and the `RecursiveSpinlock`. There is also a `Semaphore` type available, which can be used as a counting `Semaphore`.

The following code shows how to use a `Semaphore`, if, for example, we want to run our `serialpi` function once on each thread, but want to limit it to 2 simultaneous executions. Other threads will wait until the earlier executions finish:

```
julia> const s = Base.Semaphore(2);

julia> @threads for i in 1:nthreads()
          Base.acquire(s)
          r = pi_serial(10_000_000)
          Core.println("Calculated pi = $r in Thread $(threadid())")
          Base.release(s)
       end
```

We mentioned earlier that I/O is not currently thread-safe in Julia. This also means that you cannot use the `println` function to output values for debugging or introspection while writing multithreaded code. However, the `Core.println` function is low-level primitive, which is safe to use from within threads.

Threads and GC

When writing multithreaded programs, it is important to realize that Julia's garbage collector does not run in threaded mode. Any garbage collection activity will block all threads, and thus can show large percentage slowdowns in multithreaded code. It is best not to do large allocations inside threads.

Similarly, Julia's compilation and type inference mechanisms are not thread-safe. Any compilation will block all threads from running. So, it is important to ensure that any code loading and compilation does not happen in multithreaded code.

Threaded libraries

In this chapter, we have shown you how to write multithreaded code to make full use of modern computers with multiple CPU cores. However, sometimes you do not have to make any effort to use multiple threads in your program. Many libraries bundled with Julia create their own threads. Most important among these is OpenBLAS, the library used in Julia for matrix operations. OpenBLAS is very efficient at using threads, and hence, if your algorithm is mainly performing matrix multiplication or factorization, you will get multi-core performance automatically.

You can verify the fact that running the following code exercises all your cores by watching performance counters on your machine:

```
julia> a = rand(1000, 1000);

julia> b = rand(1000, 1000);

julia> @btime $a*$b;
  34.593 ms (2 allocations: 7.63 MiB)
```

On macOS or Linux, the `htop` command shows us CPU usage, which suggests that all the CPU cores are active when running this code. On macOS or Linux, the `htop` command shows us CPU usage. The following screenshot suggests that all our CPU cores are active when running this code:

On Windows, similar statistics may be seen in the task manager.

Over-subscription

When using libraries that manage and maintain their own threads, it is important not to over-subscribe your threads. For example, we saw that OpenBLAS uses threads when multiplying matrices. If we start multiplying matrices within Julia threads, the total number of threads in the system will soon outpace the capacity of the machine, and performance will suffer.

The following code illustrates this phenomenon. We first define a function that multiplies a series of matrices, and returns the first element of each. We define a threaded version of the function that simply adds a `@threads` annotation in front of the loop, as shown here:

```
function matmul_serial(x)
    first_num = zeros(length(x))
    for i in eachindex(x)
        @inbounds first_num[i] = (x[i]'*x[i])[1]
    end
    return first_num
end


function matmul_thread(x)
    first_num = zeros(length(x))
    @threads for i in eachindex(x)
        @inbounds first_num[i] = (x[i]'*x[i])[1]
    end
return first_num
end
```

We time these functions for a set of 100 matrices. We see that the threaded version is twice as slow as the serial version. This is due to over-subscription of the threads, as shown in the following code:

```
julia> m = [rand(1000, 1000) for _ in 1:100];

julia> @btime matmul_serial(m);
  2.886 s (201 allocations: 762.95 MiB)

julia> @btime matmul_thread(m);
  4.082 s (202 allocations: 762.95 MiB)
```

To get the threaded performance back, we need to specify that OpenBLAS should not use its own threads since we are managing the threads in our Julia code. We can set the number of OpenBLAS threads using the `set_num_thread` function as follows:

```
julia> using LinearAlgebra

julia> BLAS.set_num_threads(1)

julia> @btime matmul_thread(m);
  2.500 s (202 allocations: 762.95 MiB)
```

When we force OpenBLAS to not create additional threads, we see that our threaded matrix multiplication is significantly when thread oversubscription is removed.

The future of threading

The entire threading implementation in Julia is currently being overhauled. It's a large project with contributors from many parts of the world. The new threading model is being built on an algorithm called the parallel task runtime, or PARTR.

The primary benefit of this algorithm is the ability to compose threads. A common thread scheduler will be able to manage a hierarchy of threads from different libraries and components. This means that the issues with oversubscription we described in the previous chapter are no longer present.

In parallel with that (pun unintended), there is an effort ongoing to make Julia's base library thread safe. A large part of that effort is in making all I/Os thread safe. There has been much progress on this front. Julia version 1.2 included most of these changes, though not all of it is being exposed to users as of yet.

While this is a significant change to the internals of the runtime, the user-exposed API is not going to change very much. The @threads macro is going to continue to be the primary mechanism of creating multithreaded programs.

Summary

In this chapter, we saw that Julia provides a simple @thread abstraction to write multithreaded code. However, there needs to be careful consideration when writing code with threads. First, you need to ensure that the number of threads you use is commensurate with the number of CPU cores you have. Second, you need to be careful in accessing global state. And finally, you need to be cognizant of any other threaded libraries within your environment. With those caveats, however, you can achieve impressive performance gains when using threads with Julia.

In the future, this part of Julia will improve significantly. In the meantime, in the next chapter, we will discuss multiprocessing parallelism in Julia. This is something that has been part of the language from the beginning and is a stable and widely used mechanism for achieving parallelism in Julia today.

Distributed Computing with **10** Julia

Throughout this book, we have seen ways of making our code run faster and more efficiently. We have seen how, by using tasks and threads, we are able to take advantage of asynchronous I/O and multiple processor cores to speed up our code. However, that is all within one machine. In this chapter, we will discuss a number of the facilities available in Julia for distributed computing—running Julia on large clusters of machines. The same facilities can also be used on a single computer for a simpler way to utilize multiple CPU cores without having to worry about synchronization requirements of accessing shared memory. In many ways, parallelism by multiprocessing is simpler than shared memory multithreading.

Topics covered in this chapter include the following:

- Creating a cluster of Julia processes
- Programming parallel tasks
- Shared memory arrays

Creating Julia clusters

In Chapter 9, *Threads*, we covered how to use the experimental threading functionality to utilize multiple processors within a single processor. Some embedded libraries used in Julia, such as OpenBLAS, use their own threading facilities to scale across multiple CPUs. Julia's asynchronous IO libraries can also offload network or file IO to a separate operating system thread. Notwithstanding these exceptions, most Julia code continues to be limited to a single core.

Julia, however, contains an easy-to-use multiprocessor mechanism. You can start multiple Julia processes, either on a single host, or across a network, and control, communicate, and execute programs across the entire cluster.

Starting a cluster

The communication between Julia processes is **one-sided**, in the sense of there being a master process that accepts a user's inputs and controls all the other processes. Therefore, starting a cluster either involves a command-line switch while starting the master Julia process, or calling methods from the **REPL**. At its simplest, the -p n option, when starting Julia, creates n additional processes on the local host, as demonstrated in the following code block:

```
$ ./julia -p 2
              _
  _ _ _(_)_  |  Documentation: https://docs.julialang.org
 (_) | (_) (_) |
  _ _ _| |_ _ _ _ |  Type "?" for help, "]?" for Pkg help.
 | | | | | | | |/ _` | |
 | | |_| | | | | (_| | |  Version 1.1.0 (2019-01-21)
 _/ |\__'_|_|_|\__'_| |  Official https://julialang.org/ release
|__/ |

julia>
```

The procs() method can be used to inspect the cluster. It returns the IDs of all the Julia processes that are available. This and other features related to distributed computing are available in the standard library module, Distributed, which we must first load. We can see in the following code that we have 3 processes available; the master, and 2 child processes:

```
julia> using Distributed

julia> procs()
3-element Array{Int64,1}:
 1
 2
 3
```

The `addprocs(n)` method creates additional processes connected to the same master. It behaves similar to the `-p n` option, but is a pure Julia function that can be called from the REPL or from other Julia code:

```
julia> addprocs(2)
2-element Array{Int64,1}:
  4
  5

julia> procs()
5-element Array{Int64,1}:
  1
  2
  3
  4
  5
```

These commands launch multiple Julia processes on the same machine. This is useful to the extent of running as many Julia processes as the number of cores on that host.

Cluster managers

Starting Julia processes is the responsibility of a component called the **Cluster Manager**. The simplest is `LocalManager`, which is built into base Julia. This is what we have been using previously when creating processes on the local machine.

SSHManager

The other cluster manager built into Julia is the **Secure Shell (SSH)** Manager, which creates Julia processes on remote machines via password-less SSH. Hence, to use this, you'll need to set up the ability to SSH from the master node to all the other nodes, presumably by setting up the relevant SSH keys. In addition, the `julia` binary must be available on the same location on disk on each machine.

Once that is set up, you can start processes on other hosts by providing the hostname to the `addprocs` call as follows:

```
julia> addprocs(["10.0.2.1", "10.0.2.2"]) ;
```

The other way to start remote processes via SSH is using the `--machine-file` option while starting Julia. This file provides a list of machines on which Julia processes are started.

The master process connects to the workers over SSH, and starts a Julia process on each worker node. SSH configuration can be passed using the `sshflags` keyword argument to `addprocs`.

SSH is used only to start the process. Subsequently, communication occurs between the master and the workers over a plain TCP socket on an ephemeral port that each worker listens on. The master does not listen on a port; however, all workers communicate with each other, and so any firewall policies must be set accordingly.

SLURM

There are many other cluster managers available to use within Julia. Most of them live within the `ClusterManagers` package, which can be installed via Julia's package manager. Using this, Julia processes may be started on many different cluster types, such as SLURM, SGE, or PBS.

SLURM, in particular, is a popular choice in HPC installations, particularly in academia. To run a Julia process on SLURM, first, allocate a set of nodes, and provide a batch script for it to run, as follows:

```
$ salloc --nodes=8 --cpus-per-task 4 | sbatch julia.sbatch
```

The batch file (`julia.sbatch`) should look something like the following. It requests a certain amount of resources (which should be within the allocation effected previously), loads the Julia module, and then starts Julia and runs the user's script as follows:

```
#!/bin/sh
#SBATCH --time=00:15:00
#SBATCH --nodes=4
#SBATCH --ntasks-per-node=1

module load julia

julia start.jl
```

The `start` script provided by the user (`start.jl`) is responsible for starting the Julia worker processes on the SLURM allocated nodes using the `ClusterManagers` package. This is done by means of the `addprocs` function, which, in turn, calls SLURM's `srun` command to actually start the processes. Keyword arguments passed to `addprocs` in this case are passed on as command-line flags to `srun`:

```
using ClusterManagers

np = 4 #
```

```
addprocs(SlurmManager(np), t="00:10:00")

#User code here

#kill workers once job is complete
for i in workers()
    rmprocs(i)
end
```

Once the nodes are up, standard Julia distributed computing code can be written. Finally, after the job completes, all the workers can be terminated.

There are many other cluster types that are supported by the ClusterManagers package, details of which are available from the package documentation at https://github.com/JuliaParallel/ClusterManagers.jl.

Communication between Julia processes

The primitive facilities provided by Julia to move code and data within a cluster of processes consist of **remote references** and **remote calls**. As the name suggests, a remote reference consists of a reference to data residing on a different Julia process. Values can thereby be retrieved from, or written to, such a reference.

 For this and later sections, unless otherwise specified, we will run all our example code using 4 worker processes (and 1 master) on a single machine. The master process has an ID of 1, while the workers have IDs of 2-5.

A remote call, on the other hand, is a request to execute a function on a particular node. Such a call is asynchronous, in that a remote call finishes immediately, returning the Future object, which is a reference to its result. The arguments to remotecall are the function name, the process number to execute the function in, and the arguments to that function. The caller then has the option to wait() on the reference until the call completes, and then fetch() the result into its own process:

```
julia> a = remotecall(sqrt, 2, 4.0)
Future(2, 1, 4, nothing)

julia> wait(a)
Future(2, 1, 4, nothing)

julia> fetch(a)
2.0
```

For simple use cases, the `remotecall_fetch` function can combine these two steps, and return the function result at once:

```
julia> remotecall_fetch(sqrt, 2, 4.0)
2.0
```

Almost all of the parallel programming libraries are built on top of these basic facilities.

Programming parallel tasks

The low-level facilities examined previously are quite flexible and very powerful. However, they leave a lot to be desired in terms of ease of use. Julia, therefore, has built a set of higher-level programming tools that make it much easier to write parallel code.

The @everywhere macro

The `@everywhere` macro is used to run the same code in all the processes in the cluster. This is useful for setting up the environment for running the actual parallel computation later. The following code loads the `Distributions` package and calls the `rand` method on all the nodes simultaneously:

```
julia> using Pkg

julia> Pkg.add("Distributions")
...

julia> using Distributions

julia> @everywhere using Distributions

julia> @everywhere println(rand(Normal()))
0.02677553766971082
        From worker 3: 0.23364232530617432
        From worker 2: -0.39529492341877287
        From worker 5: -0.5384994386775315
        From worker 4: 0.5964077647437103
```

However, before we load the code on all nodes, we need to install the package in our environment, and then precompile it on the first load. All of this we do on the master node. Only once the code is installed and precompiled on the master do we load it on the worker nodes. This pattern is very common when working with distributed code in Julia.

If your nodes are on separate machines, you'll have to install the package on each server (unless you are using a shared filesystem to store the packages). In that case, I would recommend using a deployment tool to automatically deploy Julia and its packages consistently across the cluster.

The @spawn macro

@spawn is a simpler way to run a function in a remote process without having to specify the remote node or having to work through ambiguous syntax:

```
julia> a=@spawn randn(5,5)^2
Future(2, 1, 32, nothing)

julia> fetch(a)
5×5 Array{Float64,2}:
  3.47542 1.97838 -3.37651 -0.370807 -0.402992
  1.35532 -2.29925 3.69952 0.74422 4.75399
 -0.148023 -1.50948 2.5483 0.562872 2.04142
  2.65948 0.59873 -3.55425 -1.22119 2.56416
  0.122034 -1.86732 0.172352 -1.64478 2.12055
```

This macro actually creates a closure around the code being called on the remote node. This means that any variable declared on the current node will be copied over to the remote node. In the preceding code, the random array is created on the remote node. However, in the following code, the random array is created on the current node and copied to the remote node.

Therefore, even though the two code extracts appear similar, they will have very different performance characteristics:

```
julia> b=rand(5,5)
5×5 Array{Float64,2}:
 0.293479 0.756017 0.613553 0.839244 0.975896
 0.790796 0.0258253 0.84192 0.097875 0.648345
 0.65157 0.648335 0.134 0.024933 0.347661
 0.356713 0.0202459 0.800753 0.278525 0.574208
 0.545351 0.418029 0.721319 0.427315 0.650055

julia> a=@spawn b^2
Future(3, 1, 34, nothing)

julia> fetch(a)
5×5 Array{Float64,2}:
 1.91533 1.06413 2.27475 0.98636 2.10616
 1.18956 1.41738 1.16579 0.991499 1.55884
```

```
0.989724 0.742055 1.23431 0.769128 1.34311
1.05494 1.03503 0.980425 0.64426 1.17283
1.46755 1.17114 1.59428 0.913378 1.72195
```

We can see how expensive these data transfer operations can be by timing the difference between generating a matrix in the master and copying it to the worker, as opposed to generating it in the worker:

```
julia> @time begin
           A = rand(1000,1000)
           Bref = @spawn A^2
           fetch(Bref)
       end;
  2.237205 seconds (7.65 k allocations: 20.490 MiB, 9.41% gc time)

julia> @time begin
           Bref = @spawn rand(1000,1000)^2
           fetch(Bref)
       end;
  0.648072 seconds (289 allocations: 7.640 MiB)
```

We see that it takes over a second to copy a matrix with a million values from the master to the worker. Hence, when designing distributed systems, it is crucial to consider the impact of data transfer between the nodes.

The @spawnat macro

An extension of the `@spawn` macro is the `@spawnat` macro, which is similar, except that it allows you to specify which worker node should run the job. In the following code, we execute `rand` in worker 2, but execute the addition in worker 3:

```
julia> r = remotecall(rand, 2, 2, 2)
Future(2, 1, 111923, nothing)

julia> s = @spawnat 3 1 .+ fetch(r)
Future(3, 1, 111924, nothing)

julia> fetch(s)
2×2 Array{Float64,2}:
 1.5451 1.35914
 1.30632 1.56758
```

This code also illustrates that `fetch` can be used to retrieve results in any worker. It does not need to be restricted to the master. All workers can communicate among themselves.

Parallel for loops

Julia includes an inbuilt parallel `for` loop that can automatically distribute the computation within the loop across all nodes in a cluster. This can sometimes allow code to speed up across machines with little programmer intervention.

In the following code, we generate a million random numbers and add them. The first function computes each step serially:

```
function serial_add()
    s=0.0
    for i = 1:1000000
        s=s+randn()
    end
    return s
end
```

Each step in this loop can be computed independently, and thus should be easy to parallelize. The second function here attempts to distribute the steps across the cluster:

```
function parallel_add()
    return @distributed (+) for i=1:1000000
        randn()
    end
end
```

We can see that the parallel function provides a significant performance improvement, without the programmer having to manage the task distribution or internode communication explicitly:

```
julia> @btime serial_add()
  4.508 ms (0 allocations: 0 bytes)
-1127.587226565567

julia> @btime parallel_add()
  2.699 ms (200 allocations: 8.58 KiB)
1711.033748662133
```

Now, let's have a look at the parallel map in the next section.

Parallel map

The parallel `for` loop we saw previously can perform a reduction (the addition in that code) and works well, even if each step in the computation is lightweight. For code where each iteration is heavyweight, and there is no reduction to be done, the parallel map construct is useful. In the following code, we create 10 large matrices and then perform a singular value decomposition on each. We see that parallelizing this computation can attain significant speedup simply by changing one character in the code:

```julia
julia> x=[rand(100,100) for i in 1:10];

julia> @everywhere using LinearAlgebra

julia> @btime map(svd, x);
  30.950 ms (122 allocations: 4.71 MiB)

julia> @btime pmap(svd, x);
  19.061 ms (1499 allocations: 1.59 MiB)
```

The difference between `pmap` and `@distributed` is worth considering. At first glance, they seem similar, except for the built-in ability to reduce in `@distributed`. And indeed, they do operate in similar ways. The crucial difference, however, is in how they distribute and allocate work to the nodes.

Both of these constructs operate on an iterator: a one-dimensional list or array of some sort. The `pmap` function takes the list and passes each element of the list, one at a time, to each worker node. As each node returns the result, the next element is sent out to it. The `@distributed` macro, however, divides up the list into a number of blocks, corresponding to the number of worker nodes available. Each worker is then sent the whole block upfront, giving it all the elements required to operate on in one message at the start.

So, what are the consequences of this difference? The `pmap` function is useful when the operation on a single element is reasonably time-consuming, and the number of elements is relatively small. It is also good in situations where different elements of the list take differing amounts of time to process. The `@distributed` macro is better when each operation is very quick, and every element takes approximately the same time to be processed.

Distributed Monte Carlo

In earlier chapters on Threads and GPUs, we have encountered code to calculate the value of Pi using the Monte Carlo simulation. As an example of code that can be easily parallelized, let's try to run this over a distributed Julia cluster. First, we define our function to count the number of hits inside the unit circle:

```
@everywhere function darts_in_circle(N)
    n = 0
    for i in 1:N
        if rand()^2 + rand()^2 < 1
            n += 1
        end
    end
    return n
end
```

This is then used via pmap to run in parallel on multiple nodes:

```
function pi_distributed(N, loops)
    n = sum(pmap((x)->darts_in_circle(N), 1:loops))
    4 * n / (loops * N)
end
```

We also define a serial version to compare timings:

```
function pi_serial(n)
    return 4 * darts_in_circle(n) / n
end
```

Timing both these functions, for the same number of total iterations, we see a 2x performance improvement, which is what we would expect on my computer with 2 CPU cores:

```
julia> @btime pi_distributed(1_000_000, 50)
  107.907 ms (3881 allocations: 149.16 KiB)
3.14161056

julia> @btime pi_serial(50_000_000)
  197.056 ms (0 allocations: 0 bytes)
3.14180576
```

Hence, we surmise that for parallelizable algorithms with little data transfer, Julia makes it very easy to achieve ideal performance gains with almost no overhead.

Distributed arrays

The `DistributedArrays` package provides an implementation of partitioned multidimensional arrays. They can be used to store data across multiple machines when the data is large enough that it does not fit in the memory of one machine. It is also useful when a computation must be distributed across multiple machines, and needs to read and write access to a shared buffer of data. Detailed package documentation is available at `https://github.com/JuliaParallel/DistributedArrays.jl`.

To use `DistributedArrays`, it should be added to your environment using the package manager:

```julia
julia> using Pkg

julia> Pkg.add("DistributedArrays")

julia> using DistributedArrays
```

Distributed arrays are created from existing arrays, or they can be initialized to certain values, using `dzero` or `dfill`:

```julia
julia> @everywhere using DistributedArrays

julia> d=dzeros(12, 12)
12×12 DArray{Float64,2,Array{Float64,2}}:
 0.0 0.0 0.0 0.0 0.0 0.0 0.0 0.0 0.0 0.0 0.0 0.0
 0.0 0.0 0.0 0.0 0.0 0.0 0.0 0.0 0.0 0.0 0.0 0.0
 ...
```

Existing arrays can be distributed as follows:

```julia
julia> x=rand(10,10);

julia> dx = distribute(x)
10×10 DArray{Float64,2,Array{Float64,2}}:
 ...
```

Sometimes, the creation of the distributed array itself must be distributed; that is, code on each node much be responsible for creating the array locally. This can be achieved by using a generating function as inputs to the `DArray` constructor. This function takes as input a tuple of intervals, with each interval being regarded as a 1D array with integer entries. So, for the input, `I`, `size(I[1], 1)` gives the number of entries in `I[1]`, while `size(I[2], 1)` gives the number of entries in `I[2]`.

The following is an example implementation that fills the local array with the value of the ID of the worker:

```
@everywhere function par(I)
    d=(size(I[1], 1), size(I[2], 1))
    m = fill(myid(), d)
    return m
end
```

Using this function, we can now create a distributed array as follows:

```
julia> m = DArray(par, (800, 800))
800×800 DArray{Int64,2,Array{Int64,2}}:
 2 2 2 2 2 2 2 2 2 2 2 2 2 2 2 2 ... 4 4 4 4 4 4 4 4 4 4 4 4 4 4 4 4 4
 2 2 2 2 2 2 2 2 2 2 2 2 2 2 2 2 ... 4 4 4 4 4 4 4 4 4 4 4 4 4 4 4 4 4
 ⋮ ⋮ ⋮ ⋮ ⋱ ⋮ ⋮ ⋮
 3 3 3 3 3 3 3 3 3 3 3 3 3 3 3 3 ... 5 5 5 5 5 5 5 5 5 5 5 5 5 5 5 5 5

 3 3 3 3 3 3 3 3 3 3 3 3 3 3 3 3 ... 5 5 5 5 5 5 5 5 5 5 5 5 5 5 5 5 5
```

We would encourage you to run this function yourself to get a feel of how the intervals are mapped to the distributed nodes.

For every distributed array, we can inspect how the data is partitioned using the `indices` function, which shows the range of indices that are present in each worker node:

```
julia> d.indices
2×2 Array{Tuple{UnitRange{Int64},UnitRange{Int64}},2}:
 (1:6, 1:6)   (1:6, 7:12)
 (7:12, 1:6)  (7:12, 7:12)
```

At any node, the `localpart` function will provide the part of the array that is local to that node:

```
julia> r = @spawnat 2 localpart(d)
Future(2, 1, 114307, nothing)

julia> fetch(r)
6×6 Array{Float64, 2}:
 0.0 0.0 0.0 0.0 0.0 0.0
 ...
```

Algorithms on distributed arrays must, therefore, be written to operate on the local part as far as possible. Not doing so will incur large overhead when transferring data across nodes.

In the following example, we sum the local parts of the distributed array on each node and then add the results together in the master node:

```
julia> @distributed (+) for i in 1:nworkers()
           sum(localpart(m))
       end
2240000
```

Conway's Game of Life

We saw that DArray objects are stored across multiple nodes, and operating on the local parts in each node is most efficient. However, since each worker node can also talk to all other worker nodes, DArray objects are also good for tiled operations, where each node operates on its own data and limited amounts of data from its immediate neighbors. Hence, algorithms such as convolutions or Conway's Game of Life are good candidates.

As an example, let's show you the code for Conway's Game of Life implemented using distributed arrays:

1. Write a life_step function that creates a new DArray, representing a new generation, from an existing DArray, representing the old generation. The code is split on nodes using the DArray constructor we saw in the *Distributed arrays* section:

```
function life_step(d::DArray)
    DArray(size(d),procs(d)) do I
        top = mod1(first(I[1])-1,size(d,1))   #outside edge
        bot = mod1(last(I[1])+1,size(d,1))
        left = mod1(first(I[2])-1,size(d,2))
        right = mod1(last(I[2])+1,size(d,2))
        old = Array{Bool}(undef, length(I[1])+2, length(I[2])+2)
#temp array
        old[1, 1] = d[top, left]   #get from remote
        old[2:end-1, 1] = d[I[1], left] # left
        old[end, 1] = d[bot, left]
        old[1, end] = d[top, right]
        old[2:end-1, end] = d[I[1], right] # right
        old[end, end] = d[bot, right]
        old[1, 2:end-1] = d[top, I[2]] # top
        old[end, 2:end-1] = d[bot, I[2]] # bottom
        old[2:end-1, 2:end-1] = d[I[1], I[2]] # middle (local)
        life_rule(old) # Step!
    end
end
```

2. This code uses the `life_rule` function, which, as the name suggests, implements the rules for copying one generation to the other. This function operates entirely on local arrays:

```
@everywhere function life_rule(old)
    m, n = size(old)
    new = similar(old, m-2, n-2)
    for j = 2:n-1
        @inbounds for i = 2:m-1
            nc = (+)(old[i-1, j-1], old[i-1, j], old[i-1, j+1],
                     old[i, j-1], old[i, j+1],
                     old[i+1, j-1], old[i+1, j], old[i+1, j+1])
            new[i-1,j-1] = (nc == 3 || nc == 2 && old[i,j])
        end
    end
    new
end
```

3. We then create the first generation as `DArray`, initialized with random Boolean values:

```
julia> A = DArray(I->rand(Bool, length.(I)), (20,20))
20×20 DArray{Bool,2,Array{Bool,2}}:
  true  true  false true  false ... true  true  false false false
  true  false true  false false ... true  false true  true  true
  true  false false false false ... true  true  true  true  true
  ...
```

4. A nicer way of visualizing these arrays is via the `Colors` package (which you should install via the package manager) and then load with `using Colors`. With that, we can view the array as an image in the following image pattern, if we run this code within IJulia notebooks:

5. Now, we can generate each step of the Game of Life, and visualize the result in a similar fashion in the following image:

This example shows us that it is possible to write complex distributed algorithms using `DArray`. You need to be careful as to how you transfer data across nodes, but, beyond that, the APIs are not very complex.

Shared arrays

Distributed arrays are a fully generic solution that scales across many networked hosts in order to work on data that cannot fit in memory on a single machine. However, in many circumstances, the data does fit in memory, but we would want multiple Julia processes to improve throughput by fully utilizing all cores in a machine. In this situation, shared arrays are useful in terms of getting different Julia processes to operate on the same data.

Shared arrays, as the name suggests, are arrays that are shared across multiple Julia processes on the same machine. They are created by mapping the same region in memory to different processes. Functionality relating to shared arrays lives in the `SharedArrays` module within base Julia. Constructing a shared array requires specifying its type, its dimensions, and the list of process IDs that will have access to the array:

```
julia> using SharedArrays

julia> S=SharedArray{Float64}((100, 100, 5), pids=[2, 3, 4, 5]);
```

Once a shared array is created, it is then accessible in full to all specified workers (on the same machine). Unlike a distributed array, the data is not partitioned across machines, and hence there is no need for any data transfer between nodes. In the following example, we iterate over all indexes of the shared array, distributed across all our workers, and fill each element of the array with the ID of the process in which it runs. This code does not consider any partitions of the data, demonstrating that every element of a `SharedArray` is accessible from every worker node:

```
julia> pmap(x->S[x]=myid(), eachindex(S));
```

We can inspect the array and see that it has been populated with data from the remote processes:

```
julia> S
100×100×5 SharedArray{Float64,3}:
[:, :, 1] =
 2.0 3.0 3.0 3.0 3.0 3.0 3.0 3.0 3.0 3.0 ... 2.0 2.0 2.0 2.0 2.0 3.0 3.0 3.0
 3.0 3.0
 3.0 2.0 2.0 2.0 2.0 2.0 2.0 2.0 2.0 2.0 3.0 3.0 3.0 3.0 3.0 2.0 2.0 2.0
 2.0 2.0
```

Hence, when the data is small enough to fit in memory, but large enough to require multiple cores to process, shared arrays are particularly useful. Not only are they highly performant in these situations, but it is also much easier to write code for them.

Parallel prefix sum with shared arrays

In Chapter 9, *Threads*, we discussed an algorithm for calculating the prefix sum (or cumulative sum) of an array. We can implement a similar algorithm with SharedArrays, which operates on multiple processes, accessing a commonly shared array:

```
function prefix_shared!(y::SharedArray)
    l=length(y)
    k=ceil(Int, log2(l))
    for j=1:k
        @sync @distributed for i=2^j:2^j:min(l, 2^k)
            @inbounds y[i] = y[i-2^(j-1)] + y[i]
        end
    end
    for j=(k-1):-1:1
        @sync @distributed for i=3*2^(j-1):2^j:min(l, 2^k)
            @inbounds y[i] = y[i-2^(j-1)] + y[i]
        end
    end
    y
end
```

I hope you will agree that Julia makes it easy to express an algorithm in many different ways. Whatever mechanism we choose for parallelism, the essence of the algorithm is still apparent when reading the code—it hasn't been hidden by layers of the infrastructure.

Summary

This chapter has provided an introductory look at the parallel computing facilities incorporated into the Julia language. While we haven't covered much detail in this chapter, you have hopefully seen how easy it is to get started with distributed computation in Julia. We hope you will be able to apply these basic principles to your problem in order to create scalable distributed solutions.

Licences

Some code in this book is influenced by the following open source projects:

The Julia language is licensed under the MIT License. This "language" consists of the compiler (the contents of `src/`), most of the standard library (`base/`), and some utilities (most of the rest of the files in this repository).

Copyright (c) 2009–2019: Jeff Bezanson, Stefan Karpinski, Viral B. Shah, and other contributors:

`https://github.com/JuliaLang/julia/contributors`

The `StructArrays.jl` package is licensed under the MIT "Expat" License:

Copyright (c) 2018: Pietro Vertechi.

The `DistributedArrays.jl` package is licensed under the MIT "Expat" License:

Copyright (c) 2015: Julia Parallel Contributors

The `SIMD.jl` package is licensed under the Simplified "2-clause" BSD License:

Other Books You May Enjoy

If you enjoyed this book, you may be interested in these other books by Packt:

Julia Programming Projects
Adrian Salceanu

ISBN: 978-1-78829-274-0

- Leverage Julia's strengths, its top packages, and main IDE options
- Analyze and manipulate datasets using Julia and DataFrames
- Write complex code while building real-life Julia applications
- Develop and run a web app using Julia and the HTTP package
- Build a recommender system using supervised machine learning
- Perform exploratory data analysis
- Apply unsupervised machine learning algorithms
- Perform time series data analysis, visualization, and forecasting

Julia 1.0 Programming - Second Edition
Ivo Balbaert

ISBN: 978-1-78899-909-0

- Set up your Julia environment to achieve high productivity
- Create your own types to extend the built-in type system
- Visualize your data in Julia with plotting packages
- Explore the use of built-in macros for testing and debugging, among other uses
- Apply Julia to tackle problems concurrently
- Integrate Julia with other languages such as C, Python, and MATLAB

Leave a review - let other readers know what you think

Please share your thoughts on this book with others by leaving a review on the site that you bought it from. If you purchased the book from Amazon, please leave us an honest review on this book's Amazon page. This is vital so that other potential readers can see and use your unbiased opinion to make purchasing decisions, we can understand what our customers think about our products, and our authors can see your feedback on the title that they have worked with Packt to create. It will only take a few minutes of your time, but is valuable to other potential customers, our authors, and Packt. Thank you!

Index

D

deep learning
  on GPU 141, 142, 143
default inlining 61, 63
dispatch 35
distributed arrays 188, 189, 190
Distributed Monte Carlo 187

F

flame graph 26
floating point operations per second (flops) 70
floating point unit (FPU) 83
floating point
  about 83, 84
  accuracy 84
function barriers 51

G

garbage collection (GC) 109
generated functions
  about 72
  using 72, 73
  using, for performance 73, 74, 75
generic library function
  writing, with arrays 123, 124, 125
globals
  issues 58, 59
  used, for fixing performance issues 59, 60, 61
  using 57
GPU performance
  data processing 140
  kernels, combining 140
  measuring 135, 136, 137
  scalar iteration 138, 139
  tips 138
Graphics Processing Unit (GPU)
  about 127, 128, 129
  deep learning 141, 142, 143
  Monte Carlo simulation 133, 134

H

high-performance I/O 156
high-performance web serving
  port sharing 156

higher-level programming tools
  @everywhere macro 182, 183
  @spawn macro 183
  @spawnat macro 184
  parallel for loop 185
  parallel map 186
Horner macro 71, 72
Horner method 70, 71
hwloc library 162, 163

I

immutable types 38
inlining
  about 61
  controlling 63, 64
  default inlining 61, 63
  disabling 65, 66
Institute of Electrical and Electronics Engineers
    (IEEE) 83
integers
  about 77, 78, 79
  overflow 79, 80, 81
Intermediate Representation (IR) 11, 62

J

Julia compilation process 67, 68
Julia functions
  @time macro 20
  measuring 19
  time macros 21, 22
Julia processes
  communication 181
Julia profiler
  about 22
  ProfileView 25, 26
  using 23, 24
Julia type system
  about 33
  abstract types 36
  composite types 38
  immutable types 38
  multiple dispatch 35
Julia
  about 8, 9, 130, 131
  code specialization 13

Made in the USA
Middletown, DE
20 October 2020